Good Crazy
Essays Of a Mad Housewife, Second Edition

Karen Adragna Walsh

6/25/2024

Karen Adragna Walsh

ISBN: 1499278500
ISBN 13: 9781499278507

To my parents Peter and Mary, who guided me through life with love and humor. And to the spirit world, whose encouraging signs brought this book to print.

Contents

Introduction

Humor is the constant ingredient in Karen Adragna Walsh's life. Through her collection of short personal essays, she tries not to take life too seriously. When the ordinary happenings of daily living erupt, she soon discovers that there is no escaping life's funny side.

Predicaments Beyond my Control

It's time for those towels to come out of the closet

"Towel Rage" has nothing to do with driving—it has everything to do with drying. It can strike at any time and at any place, whenever a wet face or pair of hands come in contact with a saturated towel.

Here's a typical scenario: I am at a party amongst several guests, nibbling on scrumptious hors d'oeuvres and sipping cocktails, when the urge hits.

Once inside the lavatory, I look around for the toilet paper, soap and a towel. I expect to see terry-cloth sardined in a straw basket or neatly folded on the top of a counter; instead, I find a doll-house-sized replica, clinging to a rack. Just one itsy bitsy teeny weenie towel for a multitude of guests propels me into "towel rage."

How can one towel possibly service 20 guests and do a dry job? That's 40 hands, times the amount of facility usage. I'm no mathematician, but it all adds up to inadequacy, literally pushing absorption beyond its limits. Just give me a couple of towels or one gigantic one. I don't care if it's worn, torn, jagged, ragged or says the Sheraton Hotel on it.

I've seen wet countertops even with adequate "dryage." I just want to take my 1500 watt assault hair dryer and vaporize any lingering dampness. If the wallpaper wasn't securely intact—I'd rip off a piece and use that! Then I would scribble in red lipstick on the bathroom mirror—"Replace Towel Or Die!" There, now I feel better.

Another irritation is that the fancier the faucet fixtures, the less drying material I get. Sure, the bathroom might captivate me with flickering vanilla scented candles, shiny brass, and decorative porcelain, but one measly embroidered hand towel just doesn't do it for me. It's nice to look at, but not absorbent enough to dry.

We should learn from history. Water dripping from overused towels for thousands and thousands of years may even have led to the great biblical flood. Noah and his ark were most likely spared, because he had enough sense to take aboard plenty of sets of "his" and "her" towels for each pair of creatures.

There was a reason why Elvis "left the building." I believe he was at a party, went to the bathroom and tried to dry his hands. The towel was too wet, and he inadvertently dripped water on his blue suede shoes. He got so disgusted that he left and hasn't been seen since.

Then, of course, there's the shaken-hand syndrome. This happens when I shake, rattle and roll my upper extremities in the air, hoping to fling away every last water droplet—leaving water spots on the wall!

It's about time towels came out of the linen closet. Most people own more than one towel. Who throws out towels? We may recycle them into rags, but like matter, towels never seem to be destroyed.

The solution to towel rage is not a simple one. Telling the hostess that there has been an oversight—not enough fresh towels were laid out—could offend. Many of us would rather tread shark-infested waters than make that statement. The strategy of opening the bathroom cabinet and pulling out a new towel has occurred to me. But since I'm Catholic, snooping around in someone else's things and invading someone's privacy means I would have to go straight to confession.

As for myself, the only way out seems to be to continue to dry my hands on my socks or even the back of the toilet seat cover, if it comes down to that. Who am I to say practicality is better than elegance?

In the end, everyone must find his or her own way of dealing with towel rage, whether it's wearing a turban as a towel rack or swiping some extra napkins and sneaking them into the bathroom. In my opinion, hosts and hostesses who don't provide adequate "dryage" are all wet. And, unfortunately, so are their guests.

Unforgiving blue jeans can really be a pain

It all began in 1873, when the first pair of blue jeans were patented by Levi Strauss and Co. Starting out as durable work clothes, retailing at approximately $1.50 a pair, levis have since branched out into every facet of the clothing industry. But there are limits—clothing should not talk to me, embarrass me or hurt me.

Clothing should not talk. Then why is it that my jeans are the first to inform me that I have put on extra pounds? Are my jeans in cahoots with my bellybutton? I think someone comes in the middle of the night, wets an inflation needle and sticks it directly into my bellybutton. The next morning, my waist-line resembles a basketball and my pants no longer fit. If clothes must talk, why not have zippers with audible alarms that warn me when necessary, such as: "OK, keep going, too tight, too painful, turn back, too late!"?

Clothing should not embarrass. My jeans can be devious. I was feeling brave one morning because I had been losing weight, so I went directly to my closet, pulled out a pair of jeans that hadn't fit for quite some time and tried them on. "Wow," a miracle just happened. They looked and felt great with plenty of room to spare.

I showed my husband and even some of the neighbors how much room there existed between myself and the pants. I even had thoughts of actually purchasing a belt to take in the extra slack. I proudly wore them the entire day. Then night fell, and so did my aspirations.

As bed time approached, I took off my happy jeans. My eyes were immediately drawn to an unfamiliar label sewn on the back pocket. "These aren't mine!" I blurted out. I had been wearing my husband's jeans all along. I couldn't decide from which I had suffered more, embarrassment or depression. Where is "jean" therapy when I need it?

I left my mark on the ski slopes, not because of my expert skiing abilities but because of a pair of brand new blue jeans. It was my first attempt at skiing and I wanted to look good. I knew I had fallen big time, but I never would have imagined that my Levis were actually taking count. Glancing up the slope, all I could see were patches of blue snow. Ever time my butt hit the ground, the dye from my soaked jeans had literally rubbed off. Since then, I've stopped wearing unwashed clothing, eradicating the blue-snow syndrome.

Clothing should not hurt. Though I'm beyond the diaper stage, I still fear rainy days and wet pants. My jeans simply cannot get wet. I had it worse than Houdini ever had. He managed to get out of a tank submerged in water with his limbs bound in chains. I couldn't for the life of me get my wet jeans past my thighs. If it wasn't for the help of two close family members, I would have had to have them surgically removed.

Never underestimate the power of jeans. One day I was premenstrual, eating salty chips, drinking a liter of pop and was almost cut in two. My upper torso was nearly severed from my lower body by the sheer force of a nonstretch, nonelastic waistband. "Seams" to me I had better start looking into skirts and dresses. Now wouldn't that be a perfectly good "waist" of time?

Doing the worm dance is a tricky proposition

I hate mornings when I can't even go for a brisk walk without feeling guilty. It's because of "them."

Heavy rains from the night before left the earth drenched. The perspiring ground left a lingering mist of musty soil. Yes, today was definitely "worm day."

Generally worms are good. They help aerate the soil by casting off nutrients and are an excellent source of fishing bait. As a child, I remember my father soaking the lawn with a water hose at night. It was one of the rare times I stayed up late. Clad in my pajamas and boots, I would shine my flashlight on the wet grass and, with luck and quickness of hand, I was able to snatch up night crawlers before they retreated back into their dark, underground world.

But now I am a grown woman and my sneakers have faced thousands of these critters sticking to dried sidewalks, driveways and streets. They came out in droves during the warm daylight, not because of a family reunion or religious event but because they were literally flooded out of their homes. All my walkways were totally "wormed." How was I supposed to maneuver around them?

Stepping on them wasn't an option; doing the worm dance was— move to the right, slither, slide, squirm, wiggle; step to the left, slither, slide, squirm, wiggle.

I blame the birds for this predicament. They aren't doing their jobs. They simply fly by or sit in trees oblivious to the fact that these creatures are slowly dying. Why don't they partake of a free and easy meal? Are our feathered friends spoiled with the variety-packed bird seed from backyard feeders? Or do they prefer raw juicy worms under "grass" instead of fried and dried?

In the past, I have helped the elderly cross streets and given up seats on buses. But I never thought that I would actually help strug-gling worms make it back to land. I feel this way because I'm so large and they are so helpless. They look like crawling fingers—motioning to me to come and help them. Besides, they were dealt a cruel fate when nature fashioned their heads to match their butts.

Worms don't get enough credit. They make excellent tenants. I have mowed across their ceilings and turned their world upside down with my weeding, and they have never once complained. Maybe that's because they have no eyes, ears or lungs. I guess it's a blessing in disguise that they never see an approaching footstep, or hear baby robins chirping in anticipation of their next meal.

Worried about the increasing downpours this year, I have started the "Save The Worm Foundation." I have lobbied scientists to genet-ically alter the species of which there are approximately 1,000 dif-ferent types. The worms that roam my neighborhood unfortunately have only one sense—touch. Therefore, I have requested for another one to be added—a sense of direction! I get awfully tired rerouting dehydrated worms who are headed toward yet another patch of dry concrete.

I have also encouraged the medical field to consider cloning them with amphibians. Wouldn't it be terrific for worms to be able to float just long enough until their burrows have dried out?

To my amazement, I have gotten several county fairs to hand out homeless worms instead of goldfish as prizes. They make the ultimate low-maintenance, down-to-earth pet. Just think, no cleaning of their living quarters is involved—in fact, the dirtier the better. And no purchases of treasure chests or noisy water filters would ever have to be made. The best part is that the only food they require is dirt cheap.

Having addressed several of these rescue missions, I no longer hate morning walks and no longer feel guilty, because I know that I have helped get worms off the streets.

Critters' hearty appetites trigger garden warfare

Why did I move to the wooded suburbs? It was for peace and quiet, the love of nature and of wildlife—or so I thought. My husband and I spent long hours making our plot of landscape lush with flowers, plants, bushes and trees.

Unfortunately, word traveled fast through the animal kingdom that our back yard was one giant salad bar, open 24 hours a day. Vegetables and strawberries disappeared faster than I could say, "Peter Cottontail." And in the stillness of the night came the sure-hoofed "Bambi" strippers who yanked off the tops of my Burning Bushes, leaving them broken and exposed.

It looked like the movie "Holes" was shot in our very back yard. Our once smooth lawn now exhibited bulging mounds of soil, unearthed by burrowing moles and voles. Their zigzagging underground tunnels disrupted root formation and seed beds. Maybe the bird feeder was a mistake, for it attracted squirrels as well. And when the squirrels weren't feasting on bird seed, they were digging up my tulip bulbs. Losing crop after crop and realizing the expense of replacing damaged items, I concluded that garden warfare had to be initiated. It was time for these free-loaders to pay.

I consulted with the neighbors on how they had managed animal control. One of them pulled out his BB pistol and showed me his bird feeder, which was riddled with gunshot. He hated squirrels messing with the cardinals and blue jays. I thought that was a little extreme, so I asked another neighbor.

He didn't seem to mind the squirrels; it was the moles that infuriated him. First, he tried sprinkling poison and dropping smoke bombs at the entrances and exits, but these creatures had more hidden passageways and escape routes than Osama bin Laden. When that failed, he placed a metal windmill contraption into the ground that set off vibrations mimicking rap music. The moles did leave, but a large cluster of teenagers was seen congregating.

I swear critters are getting smarter with each passing season. They are no longer frightened by the basic scarecrow on a stick. So I went to the Internet for updated pest-control measures.

The anti-aroma therapy seems to be the most popular. No candles are involved. Companies take the most obnoxious-smelling predator scent and bottle it. The good news is that it's environmentally safe for animals and undetectable to humans. Some of the ingredients include human hair, dog hair, fox and coyote urine.

If that doesn't do the trick, there are plenty of nasty, repulsive-tasting products as well. An egg-garlic mixture repels rabbits and deer. Step it up a notch and add mothballs and hot pepper. These resources can be sprayed, sprinkled, poured and hung. A 100 percent organic fox powder can be purchased for under $20, and it protects a 600-foot perimeter against deer infiltration.

So the next time I'm at the salon, I'm going to ask the beautician to save my hair clippings. And I'll be sure to order the spiciest entree at Taco Bell—"leftovers to go, please."

But it's the fox urine extraction process that intrigues me. Do they get foxes inebriated while placing their paws in warm water? Or maybe tell them a fox hunting revival is sweeping the nation and that coats made out of fox fur are back in style?

When procrastination is not the problem

I want it, and I want it now! Sound familiar? I have been guilty of this childish attitude. Although my psychology teachers in college stressed that delaying immediate gratification was beneficial to society and to one's personal growth, I found it impossible to practice. This is my story.

I can't wait: I fall asleep before I'm horizontal and wake before the alarm sounds. If someone says, "Can you wait a minute?" my response is, "You've got 30 seconds."

I force my feet into unlaced shoes and shuffle off on the back of my heels. Once I squeezed my head through unbuttoned clothing. I was found unconscious, temporarily deprived of oxygen. I'm so bad that I cook every meal in the microwave because I can't wait for the oven to preheat.

My cupboards are stocked with: instant rice, instant pudding, instant coffee, etc. I finish other people's sentences for them. I wore my car's E-Z Pass through the grocery line.

I have no tolerance for delays: Soap operas with their lack of closure would never be a consideration. Don't get me wrong. I love watching a good story on television. I can become captivated for hours, oblivious to husband and child. But anger will erupt if I'm halfway through a movie and an announcement appears on the tube stating ... to be continued next week.

Next week? Who's to say that I'll even be around next week? Now, I'll never know if Johnny's transplanted brain was a success.

I also accuse most magazines of forestalling my reading pleasure. For instance, I'm reading along, absorbing information about a cure for old age when suddenly I come to the end of the paragraph which states, continued on page 78. OK, I can wait—or so I thought. Too inpatient to flip ahead, I start reading a different article on exercising. Same thing happens, to be continued on page 82.

This process repeats itself throughout the whole magazine. Turn to this page, turn to that page. Now I've lost my train of thought.

Stories gel together and I'm not sure whether exercise helps you live longer or you just die when you would have otherwise, but healthier.

Someone once said, "All good things come to those who wait." Sorry, I don't like to wait, even for simple things, whether it's hot water from my shower head, or the completion of a sneeze. And I don't like things left "up in the air," except for flying machines and birds.

Therefore, if I wake up in the middle of sleep and a dream doesn't have an ending, I'll lie there until I construct one.

Of course, sometimes there is a positive side to delay. Once I was in the middle of a heated argument with my husband when the door bell rang. Glaring at him, I said, "We'll continue this discussion later." I couldn't believe I just said that. But, by the time we were alone again, we had forgotten what we were arguing about.

Does phone search have to be so frustrating?

I totally lose it, whenever I can't find what I'm looking for. I start out calm and confident that I will come up with the missing item. I first initiate a search looking in the most likely places and eventually proceed to the hard-to-reach or nasty places—under the couch, between the washer and dryer.

Having watched enough detective movies, I pride myself on the ability to come up with said item. If it happens to be car keys that are missing, I would often retrace my steps. Once I ended up back at the dealership where I had purchased the car three years ago. I will not accept defeat easily. For example, if I happen to lose enough single earrings, I would simply get my ear lobe pierced again to accommodate the missing links.

I also have a long list of accomplishments, such as finding lost children in department stores and on baseball diamonds. I can even pick out four-leaf clovers amongst the greenest greenery, not that they consider themselves missing or even want to be found. But what irks` me the most is not being able to find a phone number in the telephone book.

In the phone book, there are megaheadings and subheadings modernized so as to totally confuse me. I needed to inform New York State of an address change on my driver's license. The back of the license said to notify the department. Do you think they included a convenient phone number? No. So out came the handy time-saving phone book.

I started with the heading of cars, which proved antiquated, then automobile, then vehicle, then back to the horseless carriage and the wheel. Still no luck! I even tried the talking phone book. It was talking all right, but saying things like, "You stupid imbecile."

Is it possible that the people who wrote the phone book are also the same individuals who came up with the idea of "Where's Waldo"? An hour later, I'm cursing and crumbling pages. I never did find the number, but I did find several new ways of expressing anger.

Desperate, I considered calling the crisis hotline, which was plainly listed at the beginning of the phone book in big bold letters. How appropriate. The crisis hotline might serve a two-fold purpose. First, it might diffuse my rage, and second, it might take pity and look up the phone number for me.

Sometimes, there are things that I have lost and never want to find again. For instance, the five pounds I sweated off tearing up the phone book—only kidding. The television's remote control wouldn't be a bad idea staying lost under the couch cushions. Please don't tell my husband.

As a kid, I was fearless—walking across the top of the monkey bars without hanging on, sledding down snow-covered hills standing up. But now I'm glad that I have lost the ability of stomaching amusement park rides. They have grown so monstrous and treacherous that I have completely lost my nerve.

All things considered, I still haven't lost any of my magic. I still manage to pull out from under my sleeve a static-free dryer sheet whenever I'm on vacation. These sheets, though born in the United States, have performed in Paris and in Rome.

OK, so I still haven't found that phone number or found a way from keeping frozen objects from flying out of my freezer or removing yogurt lids without splattering. But I did find a way to vent, and I hope that I never lose my enthusiasm for writing.

How would we get by without all those signs?

I've been bombarded with signs all my life. And it's a good thing, because where would I be without street labels? Lost, that's where.

According to Webster's dictionary, a sign conveys information. I've encountered the obvious, the amusing, the abusing and the not so obvious. Some are a welcome relief. As a frequent Thruway traveler, I am always appreciative of "Restroom 3 miles ahead." But what's with the "Falling Rocks Zone"? Am I supposed to duck, or try to catch them?

I cringe every time I read this sign posted in restaurant bathrooms: "Employees must wash hands." Do I really want to order food after reading that? Is there such a thing as toilet police? With guns drawn, will they shout, "Put your hands under the faucet!"?

Some signs make me feel good and others put me on the defensive. A thank you goes out to all those good Samaritans who have stuck an "out of order" sign on malfunctioning vending machines. You have saved me tons of change and frustration.

"Wet Paint" notices taped to furniture are a plus, but I can't resist the temptation to decipher the degree of wetness.

Looking back, I've had my run of bird signs. My first was the stork, announcing the birth of my daughter. Then came a flock of pink flamingos decorating my lawn on my 40th birthday.

With advancing years, I've become more safety-conscious. I'm tempted to stake "Beware of Dog" or "Beware of Attack Rabbit" signs to ward off suspicious characters. And if that doesn't work, I'll make my own, "Beware of teenager."

A car's rear bumper has been the host of many stickers from the patriotic "God Bless America," to the coarser, "Unless you're a hemorrhoid, get off my ..."

Some signs are costly in terms of time and money. For example, waiting in line at the auto bureau and neglecting to read the fine print, "License renewal line (last names beginning with a silent G only)." And then there are the signs that are easy to misinterpret, such as "Alternate side street parking, Mon. Wed. and Fri. from 2 to 4 except: odd numbered days, full moons, trash and snow removal."

I'm especially wary of coupon specials, "Sale, take an additional 50 percent off all red ticketed items, valid Fri. through Sun. excludes fine jewelry, better jewelry, designer collection and stores located on the planet Earth."

"Buy one get one free," is always a pleasant surprise. Then there are the advertisements that stipulate they are free but end up costing me dearly, such as "Free kittens" and "Free fruitcake with the purchase of a Ford Explorer."

Since I've been exposed to all kinds of signs, why not receive the ultimate. So I asked God to send me one himself. It happened one brisk snowy morning. I was out walking and boldly asked God for blessings. I said, "Pile it on, give it to me, sock it to me, sock it to me, sock it to me." Then I thought to myself, OK, God, if you are really listening ... show me a ... As I proceeded a few feet ahead, my eyes glanced at an object lying in a snowbank. It was a sock.

Unwanted guests spoil maiden launch

As I reflect back, I missed early warning signs of infiltration in my garage. Such as: watching my dog stare at a spot behind the beer refrigerator, discovering chunks of material missing from my knee pads and dismissing droppings in the garage cupboards as black rice.

With blue skies, 70 degrees and no wind, I pulled my new kayak from the garage and decided to go kayaking with my girlfriend Nancy. Of course, I took the necessary precautions: life jackets, a bottle of wine and a cell phone. What could possibly go wrong?

Turning 60, I wanted something different, something fun, so I ordered an inflatable kayak online. My husband and I love the outdoors and needed a toy gentle on our knees and shoulders. An inflatable kayak seemed like a reasonable solution. Weighing less than 35 pounds, I could easily throw it in the back of the car. It came with a foot-powered air pump, which inflated the kayak in only eight minutes. Also included were two inflatable seats, two paddles, a repair kit and a storage bag. I thought I was prepared. Not so.

I threw all of the equipment into the trunk and proceeded to pickup my girlfriend to spend a quiet day paddling through the calm waters of Ellicott Creek Park. We pulled up, unloaded the car and reached the creek's bank. I removed the virgin kayak from its storage bag and unfolded it. "What in the XYZ?"

As I unraveled the kayak, a nest of debris appeared. Shreds of string and material from old rags encompassed the pile. Then I saw the holes. Yes, that's right, gaping holes in the bottom of my new kayak. The repair kit wasn't adequate enough to cover the wide gaps. Therefore, I literally blew up, instead of my kayak.

I had bought the kayak for $300, so I didn't think this had been a cheesy purchase. But I had guessed wrong, because some "dirty rat" ate its way through the canvas bag and through my two-week old kayak.

A lesson to be learned; I should not have stored bird or grass seed in an open, chewable container in the garage. That's an open invite to any rodent that is both hungry and looking for a warm place to bed down. This embraces every critter in the universe that isn't a pet. I might as well have put up a "welcome wagon" sign: free eats and shelter for as long as you want, compliments of an ignorant homeowner.

The good news is the perpetrators were caught. Mouse traps were purchased and the bait of cheese was set. After a few days, mommy, daddy and a close relative were—how can I put this gently? —murdered.

A few days passed and the guilt settled in. A sudden case of remorse came over me when tiny baby mice appeared out of the woodwork. I mean they were crawling around on the garage floor looking for their parents. Apparently there was a nest hidden in a corner of the garage. Mortified, I gave them cheese, peanut butter and water and placed the mice in the hollow of a tree set in the woods. If the mice decide to relocate, they will be surprised that our garage will no longer accept freeloaders.

All seeds are now stored in mouse-proof containers. I feel pretty confident, because our next kayak will be housed in a basement vault next to a kitty litter box. I guess I should hurry up and purchase the vault and the cat before the first snowfall. Sorry dog.

Computer crashes and burns leave scars

Do not, I repeat, do not let computers into your home unless you live in a basement apartment, own a liquor cabinet, are mentally stable and have the patience and tolerance of a saint.

Come to think of it, I've never known a saint who owned a computer. And that's a good thing because they probably would have been kicked out of their religious circle due to all the cursing.

Why would I purchase a complex machine when I still have trouble swiping my grocery discount-card? A CIA wannabe I'm not. I can't remember my own phone number, let alone keep track of all those screen names and secret passwords necessary to connect to the Internet.

Having gone through the password entry name list of all my live pets, I ended up at my hamster's name. He died in 1965. Was he called Stinky or was it Lucky?

Computers are worse than television. They are monster-sized remote controls minus the couch, with no concept of time or place. For example, I'm working diligently at the computer, suddenly it's four hours later, my butt is numb, the dog didn't get exercised and dinner hasn't been started.

At least with television, I was frequently interrupted by sex-laced commercials, which helped remind me of my awaited unattractive household chores.

Electric blankets and power tools have warning labels that alert the customer of possible safety hazards. My computer didn't come with advice regarding mental health issues, although there was a note that said to save the box it came in, just in case you have to send it back to the manufacturer. That should have been my first clue.

My daughter can't use the excuse anymore that her dog ate her homework since it's mostly done on the computer. Although she did try "my dog ate my computer." It didn't fly. School rules only allow power failures with blackouts as justification for missing homework.

Why do I dislike computers? It's the fact that I have only myself to blame for mistakes, and the options are overwhelming. They took all the people in the world that had once uttered, "Can I help?" and put their advice into my computer. When I goof, thousands upon thousands of help screens are at my disposal.

My version of the help screen is "Help!" followed by a scream. Here's where the liquor cabinet comes in handy, since I just spent more time on "help" than I did writing an entire four-volume book!

The mistake key, otherwise known as delete, is way too nice of a word. That button should be replaced with a vocal outburst such as—"oh, s---."

The first time my computer crashed, I didn't break any bones but I did suffer irreversible emotional trauma. Renting another computer while mine is getting repaired isn't an option. All my personal stuff was gone, erased. I was lost in space.

Computers are harder to fix than humans? Can someone explain to me how a computer, an inanimate object without fingers, can pick up worms and viruses?

Literature in the health fields has stated that owning a dog can add five years to one's life. I'm waiting for the report that states, "owning a computer reduces longevity by five years." With that announcement, to even the score, I'll be going out to get myself another dog.

Celebrities bring out the silly side of me

Through the years, I have come in contact with famous people and it has caused me to perform "random acts of foolishness."

All etiquette went out the window when I met Richard Nixon, prior to his presidency. I was in the Washington, D.C., area on vacation at that time. His presence attracted a small cluster of reporters and fans. With my heart pounding, I broke into a circle of flashing camera lights and microphones thinking, this could be my one and only chance to get close.

As Nixon was conversing with a fellow Texan in the crowd, he extended his arm to shake the man's hand. That's when I interceded. Let this be known, "I am not a crook." Well, maybe just a little, because I stole Nixon's hand right then and there. While his hand was still in midair, I grabbed it and shook it instead of that poor Texan.

I'll never forget the dirty look the soon-to-be president of the United States gave me. I cannot tell a lie, I left embarrassed by my actions, attributing it to being "caught up in the moment." And when Nixon became president, and Watergate broke, all I could think of was pardon me—pardon you.

Another encounter happened in the early 1980s, when I met Burt Reynolds. He and Goldie Hawn were filming the movie "Best Friends" in Buffalo. After work, I just happened to show up at the movie set hoping to get a glimpse of Burt. I was able to take a photo of him in the distance. A few weeks later I had the picture with me when I revisited the movie site once again. No, I'm not a stalker.

As luck would have it, I caught Burt and Goldie coming out of a house separated from the fans by only a flimsy piece of yellow tape. I felt like a schoolgirl high on hormones. I immediately bypassed Goldie and ran up to Burt. You must take into consideration that I was in my 20s and single. Surely Burt would come to his senses and realize that I had more to offer than Dinah Shore, Sally Field and Loni Anderson.

I pushed the envelope and asked him for a kiss. He leaned in and I planted one on his cheek. It was a memory-foam experience because my lips literally sank into the softest skin texture I have ever felt. A close second would have been a baby's butt; no offense, Burt.

Not satisfied with one kiss, I craved more. With the picture of him in my hands, I asked him if he would sign the back of the photo. He said, "yes" and smiled. Shaking, I rummaged through my purse and came up with a pen. As Burt proceeded to sign, he looked at me with those big brown eyes and said, "Honey, your pen doesn't write." My life flashed before me. Well almost.

Then Burt came to my rescue by announcing that he would take the photo aboard his RV and return it to me with his autograph. Soon afterward, a man brought the picture out to me signed by Burt. Well, I hoped it was really Burt's autograph and not the van driver's.

At any rate, I kissed the back of the photo, which left a huge red lipstick mark. Now, I had a permanent impression of Burt along with his DNA sealed with a kiss and bragging rights. And I let it be known to all my friends, especially my next date, that Burt Reynolds was the last person I had kissed.

To this day, I can't recall that date's name or his kiss. But I'll never forget kissing Burt.

A Valentine's message from 'the other side'

My father passed away from Alzheimer's disease. One of his hobbies was building replicas of cannons out of discarded parts. That's how he got nicknamed, "Cannon Ball Pete." He also had a coin collection and loved to play pinochle and poker.

So when a psychic told me, "Your father comes to you in cards and coins," I anxiously awaited for a sign.

My father, having lived through the Great Depression, was forever telling us: "Look down, you might find some money." Finding a few pennies would bring us treats at Tony's, a candy store near our large house on the West Side of Buffalo.

My parents had lived in the upper dwelling and rented the remaining apartments to tenants. By third grade, my family had sold the property and we moved closer to Dad's factory job at the Ford Stamping Plant, south of the city.

A former high school classmate of mine named Eileen, along with my sister Mary Ellen and my brother Peter, were taking art classes together. As fate would have it, Mary Ellen was painting our old house on canvas. She hadn't been born yet when we had lived there, but she had always appreciated the architectural design and the stories we had told her.

When Eileen walked by and glanced at the painting, she immediately said, "I know that house."

"You do?" said Mary Ellen.

Eileen replied: "Isn't that a house on Elmwood Avenue?"

My sister explained that it was the house her siblings had lived in many years ago on Elmwood.

Eileen had recognized the house because friends of hers now owned it. My siblings and I had always dreamed of revisiting our childhood home. When I later found out that the upper apartment was vacant, and currently for rent, I knew this was no coincidence. With Eileen's help, a walk-through happened one fine February day. Thoughts of my father were strong and I was hoping he would give us a sign that he had arrived on "the other side" and was watching over us.

It wasn't long before we found some old coins in the far corner of the attic. Could this be the sign? It just didn't seem proof enough. Remembering the psychic words, "Your father comes to you in cards and coins," I thought: So where are the cards?

Our tour was almost over when Mary Ellen found a plastic bag right in front of the house. Two unused Valentine's Day cards were inside.

"This is definitely a sign from Dad," I said to her. "Don't you get it?" It's not playing cards, but cards from Dad." This discovery was beyond our wildest dreams. We were blessed, not with aces or spades, but Valentine Day cards full of hearts and messages of love.

The cover of one of the cards was titled, "Cupid Card Factory." Inside the card, assembly lines of people were mass producing valentines. This was incredible, since my father had also worked on the assembly line.

The final clincher came when I was driving home, reminiscing about all that had just happened. I blurted out, "Ok, Dad, if that was really you, send me another sign."

I turned on the car radio, and the very first words I heard were, "Your mama don't dance and your daddy don't rock and roll."

I was blown away. The message was loud and clear.

"Thanks, Dad - I mean Cannon Ball Pete. I love you, too."

Perils of Society

Downsizing is affecting life in strange, new ways

Beware, the age of downsizing is upon us. I've experienced this phenomenon in almost every aspect of my life. Conserve, save, cut corners, cut cost—that's the message I'm getting. That's the future. Don't get me wrong, I'll do my part but don't ask me to like it.

As a child, I was a natural-born conservationist. Didn't I save my wad of gum by sticking it underneath my chair to be used over and over again? Also, there were hundreds of times when I conserved on paper products by wiping my hands on my shirt instead of a napkin. As I got older, I learned that this wasn't enough. Now, litter goes in the trash. Cans and bottles get deposited in recycling bins.

I am definitely more energy and waste efficient. House lights are turned off when not in use. And I don't complain when I have to flush my low water capacity toilet three times.

I am also the proud owner of a sheet of aluminum foil dating back to 1976. After every use, I rewash it, straighten out the wrinkles and place it back in the drawer. The reason I do this is not just environmental, but because my mother did it.

OK, let me get down to business, I need to economize. This is not easy for a person who once thought that a carpool was a place where cars went swimming, but I'll try. I have noticed that food and gasoline are getting more and more expensive, so I have taken steps to cut costs. I'll go out of my way, five miles if I have to, in order to find a gas station with the cheapest prices. And with clipped coupons aboard, I'll drive to three different supermarkets for the best bargains.

Sometimes I try so hard on perfecting my money management skills that it backfires on me. I thought planting a vegetable garden would take a big bite out of my grocery bills. It was a great plan, but the vegetables forgot to follow through. First, they started to wither and turn yellow. Then their leaves dropped off. Was it not enough water, too much, or bugs?

Three bags of fertilizer later and a healthy dose of bug juice, the plants stopped growing altogether. For the money I spent killing eight tomato, six green pepper and four zucchini plants, I could have easily opened a chain of vegetarian restaurants.

What's really scary are the effects of cutting corners at the work place. As fellow employees leave for whatever reasons, they aren't being replaced. Staffing is down but my work load is up. Promotion are far and few between and getting a raise might mean relocating from the second floor to the third. The luxury of a free daily newspaper has stopped. When the coffee follows suit, so do I.

There is no quick fix to the downsizing dilemma. But I have come up with some ways of lessening its effect, incorporating the old phrase, "make the most of what you've got." Because I live in the southtowns, I have considered opening up a snow farm. Here, I would collect and preserve snow to sell to the movie making business for creation of wintry scenes.

Off season, I would crawl around my attic and resurrect ugly antiques and have them appraised. You never know. I've even pull out my loose change from beneath my bed, hoping to find valuable old coins. If the newly found coins aren't worth anything to antique dealers, they will get deposited into the casino's penny slots. Wish me luck.

Corporations don't realize the pain caused by relocation

Corporate America, I hate you. Upon tightening their belts, companies have downsized and relocated their employees. Families have been uprooted from their homes, separated from friends and relatives, forced to settle in unfamiliar surroundings. I have moved eight times in 12 years.

This has led to a predicament I call "Relocation Syndrome."

Warning: The symptoms are not pleasant. They are stress, stress, and more stress, derived largely from too many changes happening at once. Maybe my total number of moves won't make it into the Guinness Book of World Records, but I could write volumes on stress. Stress is a catalyst that could bring a woman on the verge of menopause right into menopause.

Stress could make a women switch from electricity to gas, just so she can have the option of putting her head in the oven.

Every time I have moved, a piece of me was left behind. I now stand 3 feet 4 inches tall, and I'm slowly shrinking into oblivion. Everything is different except my husband and child. My husband's name is still Frank and my daughter's name is still Kara, but all the intersections have different names and all the known routes to essential places, like the post office, hairdressers and supermarkets were left behind at my previous residence.

What ground can be more foreign than a new supermarket chain? Not only do I get lost at intersections, but now aisles as well. I find myself asking constantly: "Where is this?" and "Where is that?" Most importantly, I find myself asking: "How do I get out of the store?" Now I know why criminals prefer robbing heavily armed banks over grocery stores. It's not the money, it's the layout. I feel like a rat in a maze, trying to find the cheese down 16 different aisles.

Through trial and error, I've gotten smarter. I now pick another shopper about the same age, stature and number of kids in her cart. I follow closely behind. Whatever item she grabs, I grab. Hopefully, I will arrive home in record time with the basic food groups covered: cereal, milk, bread, pizza, hot dogs and beer.

I must admit, I'm envious of food—at least it has a shelf life. It knows exactly when it is going to be replaced. Some of my friends have come close to filling a missing-person's report on me. My residence has been crossed out in address books so many times, it would take a detective to figure out my present whereabouts. I consider myself not permanent enough for ink and have kindly suggested that I be penciled in from now on.

When people ask me why I have moved so many times, I lie. Tired of repeating the same old excuse, "I'm moving because of my husband's job," I resort to creative fabrication. I'll say things like: "My family is in the Federal Witness Protection Program," or "It's the only way my furniture gets to travel."

I have come to the conclusion that no matter where I move to or move from, there is no escaping myself. My body moves with me. Therefore, I whine all I want. The simple act of complaining is a cure in itself. It makes me feel better. I am moving my anger from within me, out my fingertips and onto paper. And as we all know, paper comes from trees, and trees have roots, and that's all I ever really wanted.

By the time I finally get settled into yet another new home, I begin to have a nagging feeling that Relocation Syndrome will strike again. Will I move a ninth time? If Corporate America has its way, I probably will. I can only hope that Corporate America has read this article and will finally understand that relocation is no vacation!

It appears our house doesn't want us to go

My husband and I have decided to downsize our two-story home to a smaller one, with less maintenance and fewer stairs. Little did we realize that our house took offense to this.

My first clue should have been when a female police officer pulled me over a short distance from the house. The officer observed me rolling through a stop sign and then speeding. I rambled on that I had just finished posting our house for sale on the Internet and that I was on my way to the builder's office to put a deposit on securing a lot for a new home.

The officer could tell I was in a state of heightened excitement, which probably led to my excitable gas pedal experience. Fortunately, she wrote a ticket for only the stop sign offense. But this was just the beginning of signs that our house knew we were taking steps toward moving and was seeking revenge.

We eventually listed with a local real estate agent. As soon as a big "For Sale" sign went up on the front yard, things started happening beyond my control. For example, my daughter spilled not just a few chunks of salsa on her bedroom carpet, but the whole jar. My anguish grew from mild to medium to hotter than hell.

Then light bulbs started popping. And I'm not talking about the easy-to-reach bulbs, but the ceiling fan light bulbs.

Next, my daughter's canopy fixture, which has been peacefully residing above her headboard for years, came crashing down. I'm thinking: House, please, not my firstborn.

A few days later, the real estate agent informed us that some of her "For Sale" signs had gone missing. And the night before our open house, the coil from the garage door broke. Shortly after that, the hot tub, which we are including in the sale of the house, also broke. Critters on our property wiggled between some loose boards and chewed the electrical wiring. That was a $90 house call for a five-minute tape job.

What could possibly shake us up more? Wait. During the afternoon, while my daughter was sitting at her computer, it started shaking. Yep, an earthquake reported miles away sent tremors throughout the house.

Our house was even clever enough for cyberspace. One day our frazzled real estate agent called to warn us that there was an Internet scam on our house. Some scam artist, posing as us, posted pictures of our home and other information on a popular Web site, offering to rent our house for $1,200 a month. Prospective renters were to mail their deposits to the con artists' account. Their excuse for not showing the house in person was that they were out of town. We called the authorities and removed the listing. Crooks beware, don't try this at my home again. The FBI is on to you!

Weeks passed, and the house still hasn't gotten any nibbles. Contemplating an exorcism, I chose to call upon the saints instead. My brother lent me a statue of St. Joseph which, according to

Catholic belief, helps people sell their homes. The trick is, you have to bury the statue in the ground, either face up or upside down, facing toward the house or away from it, depending if you bury the statue in the front yard or the back yard. Needless to say, I had to rebury St. Joseph three times, once because my husband wanted to plant geraniums in his spot and twice because I couldn't remember which way I left him facing.

Who's winning? So far the score is: House 4, Saints 2.

Robber stole my GPS, not my humor

On short notice, I was invited to fill in for the quest speaker at a women's social club in downtown Buffalo. Being a suburbanite and unfamiliar with the area, I relied on my newly purchased portable global positioning system to deliver me to the correct address.

I was able to procure this engagement because last year, I self-published a book titled, "Good Crazy, Essays Of A Mad Housewife." The book is actually a collection of 20 essays which were previously published in the My View section of the Buffalo News.

As a self-published author, marketing fell on my shoulders, so I held several book-signing events at local bookstores and coffee-houses. But this time was different. What a nice feeling to know that someone had contacted me instead of vice versa.

This was indeed a very prestigious occasion because: I would be treated to a free lunch, I was the guest of honor and entitled to the guest speaker's parking space and, most importantly, I was getting paid. I felt like I had hit the big times.

Of course, with my new popularity there came new challenges. This time I would be speaking from a real microphone, not the one from my daughter's karaoke machine.

Also, I would be required to talk in front of a large audience of about 100 total strangers, not the 5 to 10 close family members and friends I was accustomed to.

The day went quickly. I read, and people laughed and even clapped. A very profitable and successful adventure it was, or so I thought. A dozen copies of my book were sold and it seemed like everyone including myself had a wonderful time. Then disaster struck.

You see, when I first arrived, in my nervousness and fear of being tardy, I over-shot the designated parking space located at the back of the building and also the attended parking lot. Since it was a one-way street, I didn't want to waste time circling back around, so I parked farther down the street.

When the event ended midday, I proceeded back to my car. Funny, I thought to myself, I don't remember leaving my driver's side window rolled down. What window? It was totally gone, smashed into a thousand pieces. It looked like someone dumped rock salt all over my car seat. And yes, my new GPS was missing.

I called the police from my cell phone, and they arrived within 20 minutes. A male officer and his female partner pulled up and that's when I blurted out, "I was robbed in broad daylight. They stole my GPS." How could someone do this to me—the guest speaker, author of "Good Crazy," etc.?

Well, the police either thought that my ranting and raving was comical or that I was on the verge of losing it, because Officer Mary requested a copy of my book.

I was deeply offended by this smash-and-grab episode, not because I'm out the cost of one window and $300 for a new GPS, but because I had extra copies of my book in the back seat of my car, and the thief didn't have the common decency to take one.

Facing a 30 minute ride home on a bed of glass, I managed to arrive home safe and sound because I took my grass beach mat I had kept in the trunk and placed it over the glass to protect my you-know-what.

Those ugly gym suits never suited me well

Before my 40th high school reunion was about to commence, I managed to scrounge up, with the help of a former classmate, one of the original gym suits.

"Oh my God, that's ridiculous — it looks like a prison uniform," said my 19-year-old daughter when she saw the mandatory outfit I had to wear. It was powder-blue plain, with a button-down collar, one breast pocket and metal snaps down the front. The one-piece suit ended well above the knee, lacking thrills, lettering, sleeves and attractiveness.

The memories of high school that surfaced weren't about dangling prepositions, multiplications to the power of 10 or the Pythagorean Theorem. No, they were about preserving my dignity when subjected to the unflattering clothing restrictions back in 1969.

Miss Byrnes, my gym teacher, was the essence of sportsmanship. I'll never forget her words before vacation breaks, "If you girls don't take your gym suits home and wash them, they'll get up and walk alone." This is living testament to the fact that, after wearing said clothing several consecutive times, the perspiration-clad suits would stiffen like boards, enabling them to stand on their own.

I was apprehensive about attending a public high school because I came from a Catholic school system, in which kickball was the only sport. There were no swimming pools or showers. And for someone who came out of the birth canal with arms and legs crossed — so as not to overexpose myself — I found going from a Catholic school into a public one a major concern.

The thought of taking communal showers with female classmates intimidated me. That's when I became the world's fastest change artist. I'd race from the swimming pool, to the shower, back to the locker and be fully dressed in record time. The dread of swim class persisted. First off, the one-piece bathing suit clung to my body like Saran Wrap, until I entered the water, where it ballooned out in all the wrong places. Thank God underwater photography wasn't popular back then.

Having swim class first period was the pits. The water was never warm enough, the towels were never large enough and the hairdryers were virtually nonexistent. Yes, I wore a bathing cap to keep my hair dry. And no, it didn't work.

You could have called me a numbskull, because the rubberized tightly fitted skull cap managed to deprive me of oxygen from the neck up, rendering a headache and forging a forehead crease that lasted three class periods later. Then again, I shouldn't complain, because the boys had to swim naked! My daughter, upon learning of this commented, "How did anyone in his right mind think that was OK?"

To this very day, I carry not only memories, but an actual part of Hamburg High School with me. Embedded just below the skin surface of my left knee are minuscule particles of gravel from tripping and tumbling during track and field. It was my own fault. It went something like this: a) square off in the center of the lane, plus b) line it down the runway with my eyes closed for maximum concentration, equals c) me winning the race. It was pathetic but then again, I was never good at math.

I was never good at dieting either, so when some of the male classmates asked if I would model the gym suit for them, I gracefully declined. Not only was that a very large stretch of their imagination, but material as well.

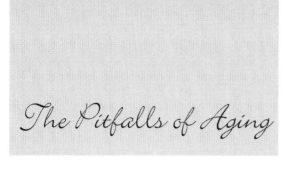

The Pitfalls of Aging

Growing old is scarier than any childhood prank

As a child, I liked to frighten people because it was fun. Telling ghost stories around a campfire was a favorite activity. Of course, it didn't stop there. I'd sneak into the woods and emit my fiercest animal cries. These included wolf, tiger, owl, monkey, sheep, cow and chicken. I always went a step further and managed to add snakes and other reptiles deep inside my friend's sleeping bags. Real or unreal, these slimy critters produced the same effect.

Halloween was the perfect excuse to scare the daylights out of someone. It was my civic duty not to disappoint. I'd hide behind the porch bushes and lie in wait for trick-or-treaters. The intensity of my shenanigans depended upon the age of the victims. Under 5 precipitated a weak boo; 8 to 12, a devilish scream; anyone older got physical contact, such as an ankle grabbing and a chase down the street.

The Fourth of July was another special event. I got to throw fire crackers directly at unsuspecting people's feet. All of their jumping and hollering brought me the greatest joy. Of course, the firecrackers weren't lit.

My mother, concerned about my ability to terrify people, lectured me about spooking anyone over 50, as in the chest-clutching category. Since proofing for ID would reduce the element of surprise, I sometimes slipped up. All I can say is, beware, and thank goodness for the increased supply of defibrillators.

Now grown up and having reached that dreaded age, I find myself on the receiving end. But a walk through a haunted house isn't as creepy as my aging self.

For example, being invited to my high school reunion when I'm 20 pounds overweight was downright horrifying. So is the request to try on my wedding dress after fifteen years of marriage.

They say, "An apple a day, keeps the doctor away." Well, the sight of a candy apple freaks me out. All I envision is a cracked tooth with my dentist away on vacation.

Even the process of drinking gives me the wiggly willies. I panic whenever I'm out in public, drink more than 8 ounces of fluid and can't find a bathroom.

Memory loss is another frightful subject. I'm at the supermarket, filling up my grocery cart, when I get this terrific idea about saving time and energy. Instead of maneuvering my cart down the crowded aisle, I leave it behind and continue down the aisle. Before I know it, I'm several rows away juggling a handful of foodstuffs. Unfortunately, the next 30 minutes are spent searching for my abandoned cart.

OK, I'm older and getting scared more often than vice versa. Don't get me wrong, I can still evoke fear. My reign of terror has simply matured with age. Gone are the physical pranks, but I've found verbal threats just as frightful.

"No television until you get your homework done." "I'm chaperoning at your school dance." "Honey, your in-laws are coming over for dinner tonight." Or, "I'm going away for the weekend and you get to baby sit." Last but not least, "Guess what comes at the end of a sentence, and didn't this month? I'm either pregnant or menopausal!"

Writer bent on dexterity bemoans lithesome youth

Just mentioning the words bending over brings to mind lower back pain, effort and awkwardness. Since turning middle-aged, I have drastically re-evaluated my bending-over based on four major factors: age, degree of difficulty, weather and the decency factor.

The age factor: Before the age of five, I willingly and effortlessly leaned over and gathered anything that had fallen: from discarded cigarette butts, chewed gum, to shiny pennies. In my teenage years, I playfully scooped up baseballs with ease; and in school I excitedly reached under my desk for love notes tossed during class.

Now all the fun is gone. With aging, the possibility of throwing my back out and walking the rest of my life at a 90 degree angle concerns me.

To prevent such a debilitating occurrence, I have followed these precautions: First off, all coins are out. Second, only a $5 bill or higher prompts any back action on my part. The government, taking into account the older generation, has issued new currency with large print—big deal. What they failed to do is rubberized it, so it will automatically bounce back up when dropped.

Degree of difficulty: I rate the retrieval of fallen objects on their degree of difficulty or physical exertion. Leaning over and kissing a baby has all but stopped due to muscle spasms. I now wait until that infant has grown full size and is at lip level with me.

I am sorry to say that my fingers are no longer nimble. The act of picking up a smooth flat piece of paper off my tile floor is next to impossible. Therefore, before I even attempt such a task, I enlist the help of my feet. I place the article between them and start bunching until it has transformed itself into a mess, but one with enough texture and dimensions to grasp. In my youth, if I didn't succeed in picking up something on my first try, I would automatically try again. Now that decision rests on "de-feet."

The weather: The older I get, the less likely I will chase after receipts that have escaped my grocery cart at 20-miles-per-hour winds. I no longer stoop to retrieve articles that have landed in muddy water or snow banks. My experience has taught me that such objects are probably no longer legible and paying a fine for littering is looking more attractive in each passing year.

Decency factor: I must admit, I have turned into a tired, inconsiderate person. Used Kleenex and biodegradable products such as food once they have landed on the ground stay on the ground. Forks knocked off restaurant tables are now left for the waitress.

Of course, I still have some moral fiber, I would not hesitate to pick up an envelope that had fallen from an elderly churchgoer during mass. Another high priority are pacifiers dropped by crying babies.

Unfortunately, the decision to bend or not to bend has come down to guilt and shame. Did anyone see me drop it? On the contrary, if it resembles a feminine product or a casino chip, I have been known to bend with amazing speed and dexterity.

My greatest fear is that when I die, I'll be banished to the "Black Hole" where all the items that I neglected to pick up during my lifetime are stored and waiting just for me. "Oh Lord, will my back be sore then!"

If your jeans don't fit, blame the other genes

OK, I've gained weight. Should I blame it on aliens for all those nightly force feedings? No. It's a flaw in my genetics. It seems certain genes have mutated over the years. My altered DNA has cursed me with the Krispy Kreme gene, the Duracell gene, the order-out gene and the bad choice gene.

The Krispy Kreme gene has spliced into my appetite control center and rendered it useless. The symptoms include cravings for fried foods with a yeast ingredient that makes a doughnut as "light as air" and me as "heavy as concrete." A strong insatiable magnetized force pulls me toward doughnut shops and jeopardizes my work arrival time. There is no cure or escape.

North America produces more than 5 million Krispy Kreme doughnuts a day and I, a faithful customer, am geographically doomed. When people notice that glazed look in my eyes, I simply state, it's my Krispy Kreme gene emerging once again.

I also inherited double Ds, unfortunately not related to my breast size, but an alteration I call the Duracell gene. I have a propensity to choose batteries over self-exertion. I don't have to get up from the couch—just push that little remote control button and the channel is changed. It's the same with the battery-generated toothbrush and the garage door opener. Energy is saved, calories aren't spent and the fat cells keep accumulating inside of me.

Another byproduct of my lineage is the costly order-out gene. I think this is a mutation of the hunting gene. Instead of seeking food, I have the overwhelming urge to seek meals by way of home delivery. Make the quick phone call and presto—a meal arrives at my front door.

There's no sweating over a hot stove or the scrubbing of dirty pots and pans. This means that I didn't burn dinner that night but neither did I burn any extra calories.

My bad choice gene is probably the most dominant one. The characteristics include never getting on a bathroom scale, taking the elevator or escalator instead of the stairs and parking as close as possible to entrances. Saving steps, choosing inaction over mobility is costing me much-needed weight loss.

My bad choice gene kicks in on the diet scene. I can never remember the right amount of servings that I'm allotted from each food group. And adding more fruits and vegetables to my diet means requesting more strawberries for my frozen daiquiri and an additional celery stalk to a Bloody Mary drink. I'll even carefully scrutinize the light menu selection, and then order a Coors Light.

In trying to find answers to my weight dilemma, I did a little research. According to a 1999 article published in WebMD, a 150-pound person, cooking for 20 minutes, burns 60 calories. Unfortunately, I also learned that sitting in front of the television for the same amount of time eats up 18 calories, reading takes 27 and sleeping requires 15.

Let's do the math: If I just skip the cooking and fall asleep watching the TV with a book in hand, would I utilize exactly the same amount of calories?

"Hello, Tony's Pizzeria? I'd like to order a..."

Game plan of golf makes little sense

"I like the more active sports — I'll play golf when I'm older," I told my husband. Well, the aging process got here sooner than I expected. So, while in my 50s, I joined a golf league with my husband this past year. Bad move. Since I am a hands-on type of person, I don't feel the connection in golf as I do with other sports.

In basketball and volleyball, I can grip the ball in both hands; feel the soft texture; and smell when leather/rubber mixes with hard-earned sweat. And when I press into the ball, it gives a little. It responds to my touch. The more I handle the ball, or have possession of it, the greater are my chances of scoring and enjoying the game.

A golf ball isn't flexible at all. I can't really hold it in both hands. It's as hard as a rock, which means it doesn't really bounce, I can't toss it or pass it and when I squeeze it, nothing gives. And the amount of time spent playing with the ball is minuscule, because the whole point of the game is to have the least amount of contact with the ball — the fewer the strokes the better the score.

The game plan doesn't make much sense, either. The golf ball is so darn small, I can't see where it lands half the time. And then, I am expected to sink the ball into a tiny hole in the ground, hundreds of yards away. In other sports, I can see the whole playing field. I can see the hoop; I can see the net and aim toward it. In golf, they have to put up flagsticks so you can spot the general vicinity of the hole.

Sometimes, I can't even see the flags because the fairways are hidden behind wooded areas and around bends. Little Red Riding Hood had a better chance of finding grandmother's house, than I, the course.

To make up for the "where's the hole?" mentality, the proprietors of the golf course printed maps on each score card, showing the layout of the land.

Etiquette, which is taken quite seriously in golf, has cramped my style. Meaning, I have to keep my big mouth shut. Unlike other social sporting events, jumping up and down and cheering are not encouraged. In fact, making small talk, sudden moves or heavy breathing while your opponent is lining up to swing his or her club is strictly forbidden.

The enforcers of proper golf etiquette, whom I call the "golf police," are usually men who ride around in a golf cart making sure the "pace of play" is kept moving. Why then, do they put obstacles in my path? The course is filled with rough high grass, ponds, bunkers and sand traps. If they don't want me wasting time fishing out golf balls hit into ponds, then why do golf shops sell extension poles with built-in ball-retriever baskets, and special eye glasses that help illuminate balls lost in thick ground cover?

On more than one occasion, the "golf police" have interrupted my golf game and allowed complete strangers to cut in and play through, while I wait. Etiquette, my foot!

The game is also dangerous. I've hit the top of my head getting into the golf cart a couple of times and have come pretty close to nailing a fellow golfer with a wayward golf ball — "fore," for goodness sake.

But the reason I stick with golf is that my husband takes me out to dinner afterward. Now, that's a course I can appreciate.

Air travel has its ups and downs

I hadn't flown in a few years, so I was a bit nervous about being unprepared for all of the new travel restrictions. But then, why should I be? After all, I'm a middle-aged American citizen, living in upstate New York, who doesn't own a gun, isn't wanted by the FBI and doesn't speak with a foreign accent, nor do I have radical political or religious affiliations. Any extra amount of liquid would probably be good old-fashioned perspiration.

It was a Friday in March 2008; I was at work, heading out the door to start my vacation in Florida, when I glanced up at the television screen. A local news channel had just announced that an airline was cited for failure to inspect noted flaws on its 737 models.

It was the same type of aircraft we were scheduled to fly on, thousands of feet up in the sky, over large bodies of crocodile-infested waters. Somehow, the mention of the words bodies and water in the same sentence scared me. But nothing was going to stop me from leaving Buffalo's cold, snowy weather for sunshine and warmth.

Before we left home, my husband said, "Do you have your photo ID?"

"Yes, it's in my purse." I felt confident that I had transferred all of my important items from my cold-weather purse into my fair-weather purse.

Arriving at the Buffalo airport, we approached the security check-point. An officer asked my husband, "Photo ID please?" He whisked out his license. "Next."

Fumbling through my new purse, I said, "I can't find my ID." For a split second, my husband gave me that "I don't know you" look. Great, my own husband doesn't own up to knowing me and I have absolutely no proof whatsoever of whom I am.

Sensing the impatience of the security officer, I stated, "It's a new purse," hoping he'd understand that things get easily misplaced when transferring items from one multipocketed purse to another. He didn't.

Then I remembered I had a copy of my book I had written with a picture of me on the back cover. I wondered if I should show him the book. Nah, he'd think I was trying to sell him one, or maybe he'd think this whole episode was staged when he read the title. "Good Crazy: Essays of a Mad Housewife."

"You'll have to go through extra security," he said.

Shoes were removed and we entered a stall and got "puffed." This meant a sudden blast of forced air ruffled my nerves and cloth-ing. Not exactly a "Marilyn Monroe" moment, but we were permit-ted to board our flight for Florida.

We stayed with our gracious friends, Tony and Donna, and had a wonderful time. Upon arriving home, I rummaged through my old purse expecting to find my misplaced license and credit cards. It wasn't there. Frustration turned to anger when my husband announced, "You'll have to call the DMV."

"I'm not calling the DMV. It's here somewhere — gosh darn it!" Perplexed, I went through my Florida purse for the hundredth time, and lo and behold, buried deep inside a zippered pocket was my license. I had had it with me all along.

So, like the Transportation Security Administration, I should have been slapped with a citation, too, for I was guilty of failure to inspect all compartments of my newly acquired purse, a definite flaw in my human character.

Try not to dwell on forgetfulness

I forgot my mom. Delegated by my siblings, it was my responsibility to pick up my 85-year-old mother on the way to my niece's art exhibit downtown.

"Where's mom? Weren't you supposed to bring her?"

"I forgot." I immediately drove back to get her. There she was, sitting patiently waiting for me and very happy to see me — like always.

Forgetful? There was the time I had signed a birthday card for my nephew Nicholas, adding my name, my husband's name and that of our cat and dog. It was brought to my attention that I failed to mention my daughter. My family chastised me, stating that I held my pets in higher esteem than my very own daughter. To this day, they open all my birthday cards with anticipation; hoping to catch me again.

Reflecting back, I had senior moments even as a teenager. A bad bowling day was one of them. My father picked me up at the lanes after an evening of bowling and drove me home. It wasn't until I entered the house that I realized I was still wearing my red and tan bowling shoes. My father had to drive me back to retrieve my real shoes.

Shortly after that incident, I felt the need to make up to my dad for my carelessness. So I volunteered to walk two miles one-way to the grocery store to purchase a head of lettuce for that night's salad. Then it happened, a bad food-identification episode. My father wasn't too pleased when I returned home with a head of cabbage instead.

My culinary "expertise" still persists to this day. For example, I got laughed at when I asked a friend how to make a fruit salad.

Forgetfulness is indeed worrisome at times, such as not remembering my combination to my work locker after a two-week vacation. And it's no wonder I don't get a response when I call my husband by my dog's name and my dog by my husband's name.

Two seconds after I've been introduced to new acquaintances, I can't recall their names. What troubles me the most is that I've forgotten the names of movie stars that I once had a crush on.

How to survive these embarrassing moments is to learn to let go. Sometimes I hold on too tightly to things and thoughts, like my 1960s ceramic mushroom incense burner. Or thinking someday my daughter, Kara, will change her mind and want to wear my stored 1986 wedding gown boxed and sealed in a $50 plastic bag.

Ah — letting go. This certainly would have come in handy when I was learning how to water-ski. After several failed attempts, I finally managed to get up on my skis and skim the surface of the water while being pulled behind by a boat.

After a few minutes, I fell into the water minus my skis. I was being dragged through the waves, head first. A screw must have come loose, because I developed water on my brain, which affected my ability to think straight.

It was only after suffering several head-poundings that somehow, sense got knocked into me and I eventually let go of the stupid rope. You would have thought that I had learned a valuable lesson, but no, the next time up on skis, I repeated the same scenario.

As I age, the more I appreciate that my body is governed by a higher intelligence. Thank goodness I don't have to remember how to breathe.

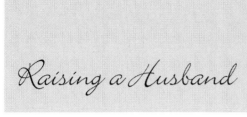

Raising a Husband

Life would be much easier if I could just trade places

Considering the complexities of being a woman, I would happily trade places with my husband—this very instant.

Shave my face instead of my legs? You betcha. No more awkward bending, trying to reach the farthest parts of my body with a razor. Without the worries of applying cosmetics, rollers and curling irons, my morning get-ready ritual would be cut in half.

Give my husband credit. He puts the heavy-duty garbage can at curbside once a week. How does it get so heavy? Because I run a 24-hour garbage-disposal service. I collect from three different floor levels. I empty bins from the upstairs bathrooms, the kitchen trash and the basement litter box, not to mention the vacuum cleaner bag, the coffee filter and the dryer's lint receptacle.

Thank goodness the overflowing diaper pails are a thing of the past.

I admit my husband does a great job keeping the cars clean on a weekly basis. But I outwash him 80 percent of the time. I'm forever washing dirty clothes or dishes. Floors, counter tops, stove and patio furniture get cleaned at least twice a week. It's a wonder I have any energy left to wash myself. That's why I leave our pets for last. I usually get a free bath in the process.

Men have more muscle mass than women. I believe it's from picking up cases of beer and 50 pound bags of peat moss. But women have a lot more stamina, especially in the area of emotional strength.

In years past, I was able to maintain a cheerful disposition while driving through rush-hour traffic, with my infant daughter screaming from the back seat. When she finally did fall asleep, I always obeyed that cardinal rule: "Never wake a sleeping child." On more than one occasion, I carried the car seat into the house with her still in it.

My husband might have bigger biceps, but I've acquired forklift arms. I'm constantly loading and unloading overstuffed grocery bags in and out of the car. When my daughter was a toddler, didn't I pick her up and put her down a hundred times a day, balancing her on my hip while climbing a flight of stairs?

Since my daughter has become a teenager, the phrase "hold me" has morphed into "carry this for me." I have single-handedly moved mountains of sports equipment, beach gear and boxes of items for the latest school benefit.

What requires more energy—my husband shoveling the driveway once a week or me pushing a loaded shopping cart through a snow-laden parking lot? I'm still waiting for the cart invention that converts wheels to blades in the wintry months.

Sure, my husband usually does the majority of driving when we go places, but I get left with the delicate stuff. In the beginning it was simple, such as delivering a dozen birthday cupcakes to a kindergarten class. So a few lost some of their frosting to the side of the box. Big deal.

I'm into the stressful part now that my daughter has reached the higher grades. I had to safely transport her science project to school in one piece. This wasn't an easy task because this toothpick-like structure was leaning 10 degrees with each bump and turn.

My husband works very hard, and I truly appreciate that. He brings home the "bread." But then I have to take the bread and make sandwiches for lunch.

Parting is sweet sorrow for unabashed pack rat

"What are you saving that for? You haven't used it in 10 years. Please throw it away." These are harsh words spoken by my husband. Should I enter a treatment center for save-a-holics? I hang on to things too long. I still have my 14-year-old daughter's first tooth, first pair of shoes and every toy she has ever owned.

My basement is a stockpile of toys, games, books and play equipment. Nothing gets thrown out, except of course the damaged items.

I've got Easy-Bake Ovens and leftover packages of food dating back to 1995. Care for a petrified brownie? I have generations of Mr. Potato Heads, who I blame for making body piercing fashionable.

Old suitcases are stuffed with Barbie dolls and every conceivable outfit and accessory. Barbie is definitely the best dressed in our family. We deny her nothing, from fancy cars, to campers, to speed boats. Her boyfriend, Ken, even lived with us for a spell. Interestingly enough, my husband never said, "Barbie must go." Why? Because of her voluptuous figure. And where did that originate from? Some jilted plastic surgeon is my guess.

Why do I save? Think of the unending possibilities. When grandchildren come to visit, I'll be able to supply them with age-appropriate toys and a playground for their imagination. And when they start to get restless, I'll give them the box that the toy came in.

Yes, I keep boxes. A discarded old refrigerator box has been transformed from a puppet stage to a doll house to a fort, depending upon gender usage, or the kid with the loudest mouth.

If you think the wall around China is impressive, think of what my collection of building blocks can do. I have enough Lincoln Logs and Legos to encircle the world. My chiropractic bills support this theory since years of bending over and picking them up has ruined my back.

Ages ago, my daughter stopped ordering Happy Meals for the prize, but I kept the miniature toys for future use. When an over-the-hill theme was needed, Fred Flintstone and Dino the dinosaur were the toppings on the cake. If it was a toddler's birthday, the "Rugrats" collection or the latest action-packed superheroes dotted the frosting.

So, you see, there are reasons for my junk. And I did let my husband keep his "valuables," which aren't half as exciting as mine. He also is guilty of stockpiling: seven ladders, 15 extension cords, 31 screwdrivers and a closet full of light bulbs and batteries in every wattage and voltage known to man. I won't even mention the assortment of nails and pieces of wood that could rebuild any Third World country.

What interests me is that my husband has recently been accumulating a stash of heavy-duty lawn bags. Every time he goes shopping, he comes home with more bags. I'm thinking—how many leaves can you have in the dead of winter? Is he forgetting that he just purchased them or is he scheming to dispose of my treasures?

It's confrontation time. He's got his stuff and I've got mine. Who's to say which is more important? So I'll tell him: "Before you do anything with those hefty bags, just remember this. I've kept the most precious thing in my life for 19 years. And if you haven't guessed it, it's you dear. Now can I keep my stuff?"

Hassle of moving takes a toll on our marriage

Nearing retirement with the plan of "less is better," we sold our two-story house and moved during a wintry December into a small ranch outside of Buffalo. If there was a reality show titled "Moving: Mistakes Not To Make," I certainly would have been a contestant.

After living in the house for only a week, things got heated up, or should I say cooled off. I was in charge of making the necessary moving arrangements. It seems in my numerous scheduling transactions for the cancellation and/or transfer of utilities from one property to another, something got screwed up.

Usually I'll ask my husband, "Frank, is it getting warm in here, or is it me?" Well, this time I asked, "Frank, is it getting cold in here?" The temperature inside the house had dropped to 50 degrees. He thought it might be the 23-year-old furnace. Turns out, the furnace wasn't faulty; it was me. Little did I realize that I was dealing with a different heating service in our new area. Consequently, our heat was shut off without any notification. My husband was not happy.

After a frantic call to the correct gas company, we were placed on a waiting list, but not the emergency list — because no one at our address was on life-support, or was too young or too old. How about too stupid? To get faster results, maybe I should have lied and said my 89-year-old mother just moved in with us and our dog just gave birth to a litter of seven puppies.

Anyway, it took a day and a half before the gas company turned the meter back on. My extremities were truly grateful and my husband was starting to warm up to me again.

Then some of our mail never got forwarded. Not the junk mail — oh, no, but the credit card bill. The bank called to inform us that our payment was past due. Having a great credit history, the bank accepted our explanation and reassured us that the problem was now resolved. Not so.

I was standing in a checkout line when my credit card was denied. I never knew that I could be so humbled by a tiny piece of plastic. I made another frantic phone call and three days later, my life according to plastic had resumed.

Soon afterward, I put my marriage to the ultimate test when I failed the crash course in moving. Our new property has a winding driveway, adjacent to two islands of trees. Late one night, as I backed out of our snow-covered driveway, my bumper met a large, stationary tree. The damage to my car totaled $1,700. The good news is the credit card was operable. The bad news is my husband witnessed the entire event. To compensate for making Frank's life miserable, I refrained from any henpecking.

Six months later, I thought things had settled down. I guess that was a bit premature because around 7 o'clock one morning, lying in bed, we heard: knock knock — knock knock knock — knock knock. No, there wasn't anyone at the door. It was a very large, hungry woodpecker pecking holes in our cedar house. I shooed it away.

The very next morning, Mr. Woodpecker returned, chipping away at our financial investment and our nerves. Not wanting Mr. Woodpecker to get an A in wood class, I immediately ordered a hawk look-a-like to guard against another attack. So far, so good. "Bring it on, Mr. Woodpecker." I'm confident that my purchase of a plastic fake hawk with my plastic credit card will suffice. At least this time it wasn't me doing the damage or the pecking. And yes, we are still married.

Raising a Daughter

"Unsolved math problems come back to haunt me"

They should have warned me that after giving birth, I not only acquired a baby but, years down the line, her homework as well. I could cope with the dirty diapers, running noses and high fevers. But when my daughter's homework started getting hard in fourth grade, I flipped.

The frenzy begins early. Even before school starts, there is a certain amount of pressure. It's called the school supply list. It was my duty as a parent to make sure that I purchased everything on that list. I didn't want my child labeled "incomplete" her first day of class.

Times have definitely changed since the prehistoric age. Kmarts weren't around corners. Therefore, cave people had to rely on natural resources for materials. Instead of a #2 pencil, they probably used a #2 stick. Mother Earth became their chalk board. And their feet dragging across the dirt served as a handy eraser. Lacking the benefit of paper, they wrote on cave walls—not to be confused with today's wallpaper.

I almost wish paper had not been invented. Humans have taken the "paper thing" a bit too far. For example, a typical fourth-grader needs wide-lined paper, a folder to put papers in, a binder to secure the folders that hold the papers, scissors to cut papers apart and glue to paste papers back together again.

Even the math has gotten harder since prehistoric times. Two dinosaurs plus three dinosaurs still equals five, but the tools have changed. Gone are the days of counting on hairy fingers and toes. We now have calculators, although not all forms of primitive calibrations have been eradicated, as witnessed on fishing trips where fish are still being measured by lateral arm extensions.

I used to look forward to having my daughter return home from school. Not anymore. I have found that her anxiety level is directly proportionate to the weight of her backpack—the heavier the pack, the greater the amount of homework, the heavier her worries.

It's the math we dread. I think my teachers collected all the math problems I couldn't solve and placed them in a secret filing cabinet. Then, years later, those same problems were handed out to my child.

I thought I had grown smarter over the years and could explain math in such a way that my daughter would be spared the struggles that I had endured. I failed.

The reason is that math has moved into a new category: foreign languages. I speak old math, today they speak new math. Since I don't utter the exact terminology as the teacher, I confuse my daughter even more. Topping that, not only does she have to get the answer, but she has to show how she arrived at it in three different ways. This has led to total frustration and tears. I won't even mention the pencil throwing.

To prove to our daughter that her college-educated parents can master fourth-grade math, we became quite inventive. One problem she was given to solve was: Two canoes positioned six miles apart are traveling toward each other, one at three miles per hour, the other at five. When will they meet?

This is how we solved it. My husband and I drove to a nearby lake, rented two canoes and placed them exactly six miles from each other. My husband entered the first canoe, set his stopwatch and paddled toward me at five mph. I boarded the second one and paddled toward him at three mph. When we finally met, the time on the clock gave us the answer. Sure it's tiring, time consuming and expensive. But at least it wasn't winter.

The tides of teen-age fashion raise tempest in the Cheerios

On a leisurely Sunday morning, the Columbian coffee was brewing and the newspaper was spread out in front of me. How I'd waited to spend a quiet breakfast with my daughter Kara. Just she and I, enjoying, as my daughter would put it, "comfy cozy time."

As I glanced across the kitchen table, 12-year-old Kara sat eagerly, waiting for a new day to start. Her one-size-fits-all Looney Toons T-shirt fell loosely over her body, exposing only the slightest hints of womanhood.

"Mom," said Kara, her voice finally breaking the silence. "Guess what? Jessica came to class wearing a nose ring."

I froze, my body tightened. How awful, I thought, Jessica was one of Kara's closest girlfriends. An alarm went off in my head. Would Kara want one too? My strong motherly powers of self-confidence and control died. The security of my own kitchen was gone. Irrational and threatening thoughts flooded my senses. What senses? I couldn't speak. Calm yourself.

It was too late. My mind began playing tricks on me. I stared down at my bowl of Cheerios. Suddenly, I envisioned those tiny rings of cereal jumping out of the milk and attaching themselves to my daughter's nose, ears, belly button, and tongue.

The picture on the cereal box came to life. It wasn't a ravenous cartoon character feasting on a bowl of cereal anymore, it was Kara transformed. A black leather jacket draped her T-shirt, tattoos decorated every limb.

She sat tough on a motorcycle. Why is she doing this to me? I was a good mom. I kept her safe all these years, no broken bones, no visible scars. Please God, don't let this happen to my little girl.

The nightmare continued. Instead of nine essential vitamins, the cereal box read nine essential evils. Etched on Kara's forehead was a jagged cross, a sign of Charles Manson's newest conquest.

Sure, I could live with three, four, maybe even five rings on one ear. But in her belly button and tongue? Yuck!

Arguments of defense started to form. Belly buttons are just dust collectors, I would say. No, not strong enough.

What about these incisions, these permanent holes that could lead to hepatitis and a premature death? Do you know what goes through people's noses? These are not nice places. These are holes to be avoided.

I shuddered when I thought about Sunday service. I could just imagine Kara about to receive Holy Communion, opening her mouth, and exposing a tongue ring. The priest saying, "Body of Christ ... Oh, God!"

"Mom, are you listening? Hello!"

The sound of her voice brought me back to reality. I stared once again at the bowl of cereal. No movement, just soggy Cheerios.

"Mom, can I have some Cheerios?"

"Forget the damn Cheerios," I blurted out. "I'll make you some nice wholesome oatmeal."

When teenage years hit, you can try puppy love

My daughter entered high school this fall, and she has started showing signs of independence. Hugs and kisses are few and far between. It's no longer "cool" to be seen in a movie theater with one's parents.

Even shopping in the mall turns ugly. "You can't wear that," she tells me. "It's so '70ish." "Don't greet me next time...just wait in the car." "You treat me like a baby." "Don't talk to my friends." "You don't listen." "I know how to iron, I just don't want to."

The dreaded curse is upon me. I am the mother of a teenage daughter. Suddenly, I'm a total embarrassment. In order to feel appreciated and loved once again, I must find a substitute, possibly a pet.

My husband isn't particularly pet friendly and I attribute this to the fact that as a child, he never had a dog. Years ago, when I brought home a parakeet for my daughter, he took one look at the bird and asked, "How long do they live?"

Three days of the cold shoulder routine. That's all it took to convince my husband that we needed a new addition to our family.

Not to show disrespect, I did give him three choices in the decision making process. They were: an affair, a divorce, or a pet. Being a wise man, he opted for a dog, and that's how Tanner, a cross between a golden retriever and standard poodle, came into our lives.

What I failed to realize is that raising a puppy is much like raising a child. They come with advantages and disadvantages.

I get barking instead of crying in the middle of the night. Fortunately, the food preparation technique and cleanup time is a lot easier with pets. Food goes from bag to bowl and is devoured in 30 seconds. There aren't any sterility concerns - no boiling of bottles and nipples, no fixing of formulas. Best of all, breast feeding isn't an option.

Not only does a puppy lick his plate clean, but also the floor. On the contrary, babies, have to be hand fed. They leave morsels of leftovers smeared everywhere, on the high chair, under the high chair, in their hair and in every orifice. And I never have to ask, "Did Tanner eat his squash today?"

Puppies and babies pee and poop quite frequently, like it or not. Potty training Tanner involves taking him out in all sorts of inclement weather.

And there's nothing like a puppy to take my mind off world troubles. I have more pressing issues to contend with, such as, take the puppy out, feed the puppy, get the puppy tired, take the puppy out.

I remember reading books as a child that read, "See Spot run. Go Spot go." Now, when the puppy pees on the carpet, I yell, "Here's a spot, there's a spot, everywhere a spot spot."

The greatest advantage is that Tanner, unlike my daughter, is always happy to see me. I can kiss and pet him all day. He follows me from room to room. He seeks my affection and gives unconditional love.

Will this last forever? To my dismay, I heard that dogs go through a teenage phase themselves. Will he be ashamed to be seen on the other end of a leash with me? Can he get too sexy for his tail? All I know is, my next investment will be a pet rock.

Teenage driver triggers a whole new set of fears

The day my teenage daughter, Kara, passed her driver's test proved to be both a proud and scary moment. Proud in that she displayed the knowledge and skills necessary to operate a vehicle, but scary in that she was now in possession of 3,000 pounds of metal, capable of speeds up to 100 miles per hour.

Since safety was always a big concern of mine, I guess practicing in the confines of a cemetery paid off. That is where I first taught my daughter how to ride a bicycle and years later how to drive a car. It was the safest spot I could think of. I figured what harm could she possibly do?

Having her drive around our subdivision for the first time with real live people in moving traffic was the most nerve-racking experience of my life. I felt like an air traffic controller without benefit of radar. She did great despite my episodes of screaming, leaning, grabbing and pressing my braking foot to the floor.

In order for Kara to pass her written test, she had to answer a question such as, "How many car lengths do you need to be behind the car in front of you?" Granted this is important, but shouldn't there also be a mandatory parental checklist?

"Do you know how to operate a dishwasher, washing machine and dryer? Can you cook a full meal? Are you willing to take your pet for a walk? Can you change an empty toilet paper roll? Will you put gas in the car?" Then and only then should licenses be issued to teenagers.

What amazes me the most is that Kara went from driving a Barbie jeep to an automobile in less than 10 years. How can I stress the importance that driving is risky business? An amusement park ride's bumper-car mentality no longer works. Hitting and bouncing off of another vehicle is no longer fun, but detrimental to one's health as well as others.

Since my daughter started driving a whopping three months ago, she has become an expert on the subject and has reminded me that my driving skills are a bit lax. I often hear, "You didn't put on your directional when you changed lanes" or "You didn't come to a full stop at the stop sign."

I first started driving 40 years ago. All I can remember is being in the middle of an intersection and hearing "honk, honk, honk" directed at me and not having the slightest clue of what went wrong.

Times have changed since I first got behind the wheel. The only distractions to cope with then were tunes from the car's radio, an air freshener dangling from the mirror and a St. Christopher medal on the dash.

Today's youth have to contend with superhighways at super speeds, a significant increase in car traffic and noise from radios, CDs, DVDs, laptop computers, GPS systems and cell phones.

Living in the snow belt, lake-effect region, I can hardly wait until she experiences winter driving. Having been caught in a few blinding blizzards, I will make sure she keeps a survival kit in her car. The basics include a flashlight, an empty coffee can with candles and matches, a blanket, windshield washer fluid, a heavy-duty ice scraper and a receptacle for waste.

I hope I have steered my daughter in the right direction, because I am no longer in the driver seat. Just in case, I'll throw in a set of rosary beads for good measure.

Life with a teenager can be exasperating

My family received an extra Y-chromosome when my daughter acquired her first boyfriend. It went something like this: "Y can't I stay out late? Y can't he sleep over? Y are you so mean?"

Even the "fight or flight" concept has changed since living with a teen-ager. It's now a fight and then a flight to her room.

Concerned that my daughter Kara's school grades would suffer because of spending so much time with her boyfriend, Jeff, I put my foot down.

"If your grades drop, no more boyfriend." Well her grades actually improved and so did his. Delighted I said, "Kara, you can have two boyfriends."

That's not the only source of aggravation. "What's so important? I asked recently, when she was almost in tears. "I'm out of eyeliner!" she replied.

I should be used to this by now because whenever I go grocery shopping with her, I end up spending more money on cosmetics and hair products than food.

The saga continues. How can I tell that I have a teenager? It's when my daughter's bathroom mirror gets more quality time with her than I do. It's when her social calendar fills up faster than a bingo card. It's when the phone rings 20 times a day and it's not for me. And when it rings, I'm not allowed to answer it. After all, why would anyone want to speak to me, a nobody, from a past generation? I might even say something embarrassing like hello.

I knew I was the aging mother of a teenager when I discovered that she owned prettier underwear than I do and that she wore a bikini that fit. Of course it fit—she is a size 0. Perhaps the only experience I have had with zeros has been with weather as in 0 degrees, zero tolerance to change, and after decimal points.

I can't complain too much, because her vocabulary has improved. She has found more meanings to the word excuse then what's listed in Webster's Dictionary. "I didn't let the dog out, 'cause he was sleeping. I can't clean my bedroom, I have too much homework. Why should I wipe off the counter? Those aren't my crumbs."

It's a good thing my daughter didn't have to write a journal on how she spent her summer vacation. Kara's diary would read: Monday through Friday – slept till noon, searched for snacks, avoided housework, instant-messaged friends, watched television, searched for snacks, talked on cell phone, went to boyfriend's house, returned home and searched for snacks. The weekends deviated a trifle with girl sleep-overs, where everyone slept past noon.

Having a teenager presents itself with little shockers. The time my daughter came home wearing her boyfriend's sweat pants caused me an arrhythmia. Of course, I over reacted. She left the house wearing shorts, the evening grew progressively colder, and so she borrowed a pair of his pants. I guess I should be happy that he wasn't wearing hers. And I'm more than happy to be washing the laundry of someone else who doesn't even reside in my house.

It's unavoidable that teenagers will have messy bedrooms. But when my daughter's bedroom started looking like the floor of a movie theater that had just let out, I flipped. My options were: yelling, shutting the door, appearing on Dr. Phil or threatening her with "You'll never see Jeff again." It worked. Anticipating a relapse, I rescheduled with Dr. Phil.

Keeping it together on my daughter's move

"Why are you here? There is nothing to do." That was the response from several people residing in a rural area of North Carolina. My daughter, Kara, was lucky enough to procure a teaching job right out of college. This meant a move from Buffalo, with a population of 270,000 to a city of 16,000. Talk about culture shock. The stores closed by 6 p.m. Applebee's was "the" favorite hangout because it stayed open till midnight.

Our empty-nest status consisted of removing more than a few feather-filled pillows. We packed our 21-year old daughter's life possessions into two cars and headed South. The cars were filled to the brim, which explains why, making a lane change at 70 mph, I nearly side-swiped a car.

We brought along two huge travel golf bags. Only they weren't filled with clubs but with two dresser drawer's worth of my daughter's clothing.

This trip was no vacation. How many devices does it take to get from point A to point B? A 10- hour trip turned into 13 hours, even though we relied on: our AAA Trip Tik, maps, GPS, and our cellphone navigation system. It seems our GPS was outdated, our cell phone intermittently lost connection and map reading wasn't one of my attributes. After missing a crucial turn, I reverted to the old-fashioned method and stopped at a gas station for directions. Like all men, my husband stayed in the car.

When we arrived in North Carolina, it was July and hot. On moving-in day, it reached 100 degrees. Typically one gains weight on a vacation. My husband lost 3 pounds. I never sweated so much in my life. My hair developed more twist and turns than curly-Q potatoes.

If moving was an Olympic event, we would have broken all records. By golly, we had her settled into her new apartment, furnished it and returned back to Buffalo in six days. Fun? No. Costly? Yes.

I should have listened to the advice: You get what you pay for. Trying to save a few bucks, we had shopped at a used furniture store. That's when the word "used" took on a new meaning. We thought we struck gold when we purchased a five-piece bedroom set made out of solid cherry for a steal. It would be wiped down and installed the very next day. Neither one happened.

Upon delivery, Kara discovered unexpected extras. The furniture lived up to its title, "used." She pulled out: used long johns, a used bathing suit and a used pair of underwear from the drawers. Kara even used words I have never heard her say before.

Therefore, our next few purchases included brand new items: a desk, a chair for the desk, a TV stand, a bookcase and a futon.

Unfortunately, some assembly was required. We are not gifted people. And it was evident that the same people, who designed the caps on medicine bottles and had patents pending on jigsaw puzzles, had written our instructions.

The outside of the box read, "No tools necessary." Don't be fooled. Sure, they included the tools, but they also included over 100 pieces of hardware. The question remained: What does one do with extra pieces of hardware that should have made it into the finished product?

So, to parents who will be moving their children in the near future, my advice would be to buy fully assembled floor models at all costs, damaged or not. The sad part was leaving behind our daughter. The much relieved part was that we left before tackling the futon.

Interaction with stars must run in the family

A long time ago, a psychic read my palm. Looking at the lines on my hand, she said, "You have several stars. I've only seen this pattern once before." I didn't know if this was a good or bad thing. Did it mean I had more wrinkles than normal or will stardom come my way?

Well, count my "lucky stars," my daughter Kara and I did get to meet movie stars. Her encounter was up close, personal and recent. Mine was only a visual, happening many years ago but just as memorable.

My daughter, with her voice shaking, called to tell me that she just met Tom Cruise. She and some of her girlfriends were at a bar in Pittsburgh, across the street from where Tom Cruise was being filmed in the movie "Jack Reacher." Not only did she get a group picture with his arm around her, but she also got to party with some of the cast members, including Tom Cruise's double and his stunt men.

Was I jealous? Well, maybe. But it brought back fond memories of my encounter with a movie star, who was just as glamorous in his day and age. I welcomed Robert Redford with open arms, or should I say hands?

Back in the 1980s, Mr. Redford had been in town shooting "The Natural," a movie about a baseball player. A call went out to the public for extras to help fill the seats of the old War Memorial Stadium in Buffalo. So, a few of my girlfriends and I sat in the bleachers amongst poster board people in the cold and damp waiting to get a glimpse of Redford.

Growing restless, bored and stiff much like our poster board friends, I decided to move closer to the action. I made my way to the ball diamond and pressed up against the fence. During a break in shooting, Robert, standing near the pitcher's mound, glanced my way. Our eyes locked. Infatuation hit full force.

Out of hearing range, I started gesturing with my hands. I curled my index finger moving it in a come-here motion. It worked; he's still looking, so I waved my hand frantically beckoning him to come closer. Placing my star-studded palm upward, I then blew him a kiss.

Robert, somehow captivated by my theatrics, stayed focused on me. Next, I grasped my hands in prayer, as if pleading in desperation for a few more moments shared between us. Then, sensing a farewell, I ended the "affair" by waving goodbye. He looked away, and all was lost.

In retrospect, I wondered why he had singled me out amongst a field of adoring fans. Upon viewing the movie several months later, I had learned that a young mysterious woman in dark clothing had caused his demise. Was this a déjà vu moment for him, since I had been wearing a dark leather coat with my collar pulled up high, concealing my looks and intentions? Visually, I had Robert Redford all to myself, and held him there if only for a few fleeting moments.

Fast forward, I got married at the tender age of 35, thank my lucky stars again. And I will never forget the first time my future husband gazed into my eyes. It was not a starry-eyed performance. We were out hiking in the woods and my contact lens got dislodged. As I pulled down my eyelid for him to locate my floating lens, he felt queasy.

Good thing love is blind. We got married. And it's been up close and personal ever since.

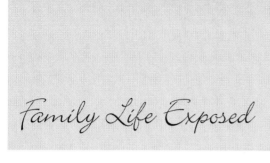

Family Life Exposed

'Curses' start to fly when you move in with relatives

The average American moves 11.7 times in a life span. Being middle aged, I have shuffled around quite a bit and have found myself between apartments and homes on several occasions. Because of the dire need for a temporary residence, my family and I have moved in with relatives. This is what I have encountered.

Underlying curses have emerged and disrupted my psyche: The Breakage Curse, the "Extras" Curse, the Mix-up Curse and the Retention Curse.

The Breakage Curse: The moment I move in, I first identify my relative's prized possessions and never use, or come in close proximity to, said items. For example, I once felt safe sitting on a seasoned rocking chair, only to discover it was a fragile antique—"set out to pasture"—in the living room with no intentions of ever taking on another rider. Needless to say, the chair crumpled beneath me, tossed me to the ground, and had to be destroyed that very day. And why is it that the one and only plate I break just happens to be a wedding gift—blessed by the pope.

The Curse Of The "Extras": Having more heads in the household means that more hairs will be shed in the bathroom. It's happened to me that in the middle of taking a shower, the shower automatically converts into a bath, and I find myself standing in 6 inches of stagnant water.

Therefore, I've learned to bring the perfect hostess gift - not a basket of cheer but a bottle of industrial-strength Drano.

Midnight kitchen raids have also led to extra precautions. I can still wear my hot pink negligee—now covered by a robe. Respectfully, and out of fear of being caught, I am always sure to drink from a glass and not from the container.

Mix-up Curse: Mix-ups often happen when one family shares refrigerator space with another. One hurried morning, my husband grabbed his niece's bagged lunch and was found eating fruit roll-ups and sipping Hawaiian punch through a crazy straw at a business meeting.

I have also underestimated "garbage." One evening I threw out a banana peel that had been left on the kitchen counter. The next day, I had to retrieve it from the bottom of the garbage. It seems that nephew Michael had scribbled his new locker combination on it. Therefore, I now read fruit.

The Retention Curse: I must keep track of a zillion things. Not only do I have to retain facts about my family but theirs as well. In the preparation of meals, I've had to memorize the idiosyncrasies of everyone's digestive tract. If I didn't, I'd likely hear: "Why did you add onions? They give me gas." "I can't eat this ... there's pepper in it. I'm allergic to pepper." "How gross, my vegetables are touching my meat!"

So far on kitchen duty, I haven't killed anyone because the "Joy Of Cooking" quickly evolved into the "Joy Of ordering Out."

Most importantly, I have learned not to be the first person out of bed on weekends. Why? Because the earliest riser must let the dogs out, retrieve the newspaper and make coffee. While I'm doing this, six individuals have already beaten me into the shower, depleted the hot water supply and clogged up the drain.

The key to surviving the present living conditions is the knowledge that this will not last forever. And sometime soon, I will be in my own home and able to drink—scantily clad—straight from a milk carton and not feel guilty.

Receiving and paying compliments is an art

Who would have thought that compliments are so complicated? "Oh what a cute baby." Clad in diapers, I didn't know what that meant, but the person uttering those words was smiling so I smiled back. Growing up, the compliments kept coming, like it or not.

There were family members whose sole purpose in life was to remind me of my ancestral likeness. "Look at those stubby fingers and toes...just like your mom's. You've got your dad's strong nose."

No wonder I kept my hands in my pockets and avoided open-toed shoes. And being a girl and having a man's nose didn't appeal to me back then, nor does it today.

It got a bit more dangerous in grammar school with the poking and the hair pulling by members of the opposite sex. My mom said that meant the boys liked me and I should take it as a compliment. It got confusing. Did he push me down because he adored me, or hated my guts?

And if a certain fellow caught my eye, do I reciprocate with random acts of affection? Was sticking my tongue out and then sticking my leg out to cause him to trip amorous enough? To rectify the pain endured for the sake of homage, I frequently changed my seating arrangements and debated wearing body armor to school.

High school offered a more muted form of compliments such as the written word. Gold stars and stickers didn't exist anymore, but there were personal notes. Thank goodness for those teachers who wrote encouraging words on homework assignments. It was an added boost to learn that one's hard work and individuality was appreciated by someone other than my mother.

When I was younger, I didn't know how to accept compliments gracefully. If someone said to me, "I love your blouse," my response would be, "It's not mine. It's my sister's. She let me wear it because it has a big stain on it."

And if someone else said, "You look great in those shorts," it didn't take me long to defuse the compliment. "Yeah, but they make my knees look knobby. And my legs are too pale."

With age comes maturity. I now welcome praise and often wonder when and if I'll get another chance to prove it.

The best time to bestow a compliment is the sooner the better. I try to be the first, because the fifth person down the line giving a compliment not only will lose his punch but also the credit. And I try never to waste. I always direct the honor to the intended recipient. I could say, "That dress looks fantastic on Laura," to 20 people but it may never reach Laura's ears.

If I follow proper etiquette, I will not dish out too many compliments. Like the little boy who cried wolf, compliments are more effective when limited and sincere. But sometimes I can't help myself. I'm guilty of the "sucking up" phenomenon. This happens when I give a compliment, immediately followed by a request for a favor.

"Honey, you are sooo much better at math than I am. So will you help Kara with her homework?"

I have learned never to make a compliment too personal, especially one directed at a teenager. "Gee, your pimples look unique. I think they resemble the Big Dipper on your right cheek."

"Oh, you're disgusting."

"Sorry, OK? The Little Dipper."

"That's so not funny."

That teenager has since stopped going out on clear, starry nights.

'Desperate housewife' pleads guilty to 'crimes'

I live in the suburbs. Does that make me a desperate housewife? Of course it does. As in all neighborhoods, trash has a way of getting around. I wouldn't say my life is a re-enactment of the popular hit television show, "Desperate Housewives," but I have come close a few times. And sometimes desperate situations arise, where I have cheated, stolen, lied, spied and murdered.

Speaking of trash, there is plenty of litter in my neighborhood, especially on windy days. I will pick up blown newspapers, fliers and debris that has landed in my yard. As a responsible neighbor, I have returned garbage pails and even mail (unopened) that has been addressed to the wrong house.

To me, the term my "Sugar Daddy," means going next door and borrowing a cup of sugar from a father of four.

Yes, I have spied on my neighbors, but it was totally unintentional. Years ago, when my daughter was an infant, my baby monitor was picking up embarrassing conversations inside the walls of someone else's home. Did I listen? At first just remotely. Then I got hooked. I cleaned out the wax from my ears and turned up the volume, because I was picking up dialogue that mimicked the "Sopranos."

My excuse for this violation of privacy was that I needed to know their identity. Eventually, I informed them that the radio frequency on their baby monitor should be changed. When the audible sounds finally stopped, I figured that they either took my advice or moved to a different state.

My morals started to falter when I went on a diet. I stole food that didn't belong to me. I became good at making false promises and concealing items. Underneath my over-sized sweat shirt was often hidden a bag of chips and the extra 10 pounds I said I had lost.

My mother taught me never to take the last cookie or piece of cake, that I should leave it for someone else. Well, when my gastric juices began irritating my intestinal lining, a name change was instituted. I became that "someone." And boy, did I lie about my weight—to my husband, to my doctor and to my health insurance carrier. When confronted with the hard facts, I said, "someone" must have done it.

It's no mystery that I am a killer, a mass murderer in fact. Fortunately, my prey is not of the human species. When night-flying insects "go to the light" in my back yard, they are instantly electrocuted by my electric bug-zapper. Dandelions get chemical warfare applications, as do some crawly critters. Four-legged rodents get the guillotine-style of torture. My apologies to Wilbur, Jiminy Cricket and Charlotte.

Guilty of the above infractions, I hereby deem my punishment to be house arrest. I should be so lucky. As a stay-at-home wife and mother, it sounds good to me. No more shuttle service, not to sporting events, the grocery store, the bank, the post office, the library or the doctor's office. Anyway, the old ball-and-chain monitoring device has been fashionably replaced with today's ankle jewelry.

Talk about scandal. I can see the headlines now, "Wife refuses to leave home after house arrest is lifted." Reasons mentioned were: the joy of knowing how it felt, having the cleanest closets on the block, and the joy of taking naps, reading books and even writing one.

Even artificial trees can be a real hassle

Kerplunk! "Was that the Christmas tree?" I shouted out to my husband. Sure enough, there was the fully decorated pine, sprawled out on the living room floor, now missing a few fragile ornaments. I resurrected the tree by attaching fishing line to a window latch.

Over the years, as my living space grew from apartments to homes, I supersized my "Charlie Brown" specials. But, feeling guilty about at the ruination of nature and the senseless destruction of perfectly healthy trees, I decided on a new adventure.

I purchased a potted tree encased in burlap and placed it in a huge tub, watering it faithfully. What I didn't realize was that the trunk and roots were still frozen and when I added water, "the great thaw" occurred, leaving my carpet drenched in tree and mud juice.

To prevent duplication of past catastrophes, I'm thinking—forget "au naturel," I'll go "au artificial." We put up the 6-footer without a hitch. Then came the lights' or should I say the blinkin' lights. I couldn't for the life of me get a string of lights to work. The top and bottom stayed illuminated but the middle remained dark.

Unfortunately, my knowledge of electricity is limited to the fact that when one flicks a switch, current is achieved. But I do recall my parents' laws of physics, which were: Don't get near downed power lines, don't drop your hairdryer in water, and don't stick your tongue into an electric outlet. Understanding the dynamics remains a mystery. All I know is that you could die.

Trees come also with an array of lights from: blinking to flashing to prelit to, my specialty, the no-lit type. I asked myself: Why is there such an abundance of lights displayed at every checkout counter? To my dismay, it's because they fail, burn out and break on a routine schedule.

After Christmas, the unveiling of lights takes place. Tired from a very hectic and festive weekend, one gently places them all coiled up and tangled back into any handy receptacle.

Once the tree is naked again it comes down - but wait, it no longer fits in its ordinal package as promised by the salesman.

So it's either find another box around the house or buy a container that costs one-third the price of the tree.

Actually, I chose another option, crude but practical. I could purchase my coffin ahead of schedule. What better place to store my tree then a pine box made out of discarded Christmas trees?

Once the tree is finally secured, transporting it back down the basement is another dreaded event. I have an elevated slab of concrete called a crawl space for storage. I hate crawl spaces. The word alone sounds ugly. It reminds me of tiny insects with lots of feet dangling upside down and sideways, which is exactly the position I have to assume to get to that cramped spot.

After reflecting upon the tree dilemma, I have come up with suggestions, which I hope someone will start working on right away. How about a device that will project the vision of a Christmas tree on my family room wall, complete with software that allows me to personalized ornaments? There would be no watering, no tampering with wired lights and best of all, no need for a prepaid coffin. Now I can rest in peace.

Stay calm at Christmas, 'for goodness sake'

I dread the holiday season because I have to go to a mall for my Christmas shopping, or should I call it "maul" shopping. Just getting into the place is a feat in itself. The jammed parking lot reminds me of an airport with cars circling around waiting for a spot to land.

Entrances are chaotic with pull-up and drop-off zones where people stuff passengers into seats and bags into trunks for a fast getaway.

No one wants to walk extra car lengths on an ice-slick lot, fighting wind gusts and snow if we don't have to. So I wait and wait for a parking space to open up. When one becomes free, I back up, allowing the driver plenty of room to exit.

The very core of my tranquility is tested when a not-so-gracious opportunist sneaks into that very spot I had selected. But, I'll remain calm; chalk it up to "being good for goodness sake." I'll even make up excuses, such as, maybe he or she just had foot surgery, or has a weak bladder, or just misplaced his or her brain.

Once inside the building, especially around bargain tables, waves of people will literally carry me away if I don't have my feet firmly planted on the ground.

Of course, the majority of selecting gifts for both sides of the family falls largely on me, the twice-a-year shopper. Unlike most women, there is nothing that I enjoy about frantic shopping but I'll "be good for goodness sake."

Ah, all those fine memories — hunting for that special doll, realizing it's the last one on the shelf and willing to take out anyone in my path, cause that's what my little girl had asked for while sitting on Santa's lap.

Thank God those days have passed. Or have they? My daughter, as a teenager, doesn't believe in Santa anymore but believes I'm his replacement, which is not inconceivable because our bellies are looking a lot alike these days.

Not one to be blamed for ruining someone's Christmas, I will divide my time and visit relatives on that very day even though I had just seen them two days ago. And I don't understand why family members don't want my 75-pound dog, Tanner, to join them at Christmas. It's not like they have to get him anything. Leaving him home alone is hard, for all I really want to do is curl up with Tanner and watch the snowflakes come down.

Christmas doesn't always bring out the best in me. "'Tis" the season all right — the flu season. Usually I'm tired and stressed, and unfortunately I'll do my part in spreading good cheer and good germs along the way. There is nothing quite like the out-of-town flu version, knowing that I have just infected a family of six before their long journey home.

When someone shows me the gold necklace that her husband got her for Christmas, I'll say, "That's nice. I'm planning a trip to an island of our dreams." In reality, I can only go there in my mind but then again, I can bring as much luggage as I want.

One year, I made the mistake of telling my husband I needed earrings. I should have been more specific. My husband hates shopping worse than I. It must be a "man thing," because whenever we are out browsing, he'll stop and admire a carpenter's handiwork. "Wooden" I know it? I got four pairs of wooden earrings for Christmas for "goodness sake!"

Charlie Brown tree is big enough for me

Last December, we had downsized and moved into a smaller home just a few days before Christmas. There wasn't enough time or energy to put up our artificial tree. The house was in disarray. Our priorities at that time were finding the toilet paper rolls, the alarm clocks and warm blankets. A Christmas tree was furthest from our thoughts. But our daughter home from college on her winter break objected. "Are you kidding me? We aren't having a tree? We always have a tree."

Not wanting to be labeled a scrooge by my own daughter, I compromised. I managed to find the one-foot lighted ceramic tree my mother had made me. It wasn't big on size but it was big on sentimental value. I was happy, my husband was happy — but my daughter, not so much. Next Christmas will be different, I promised her.

Don't get me wrong, I love trees. One of my favorite poems is "Trees" by Joyce Kilmer. An excerpt from the poem reads: "A tree that looks at God all day, And lifts her leafy arms to pray."

But I do have tree-devotion limitations. Not so with a friend of mine, who shall remain anonymous. I'll call him Stan. Every Christmas,

Stan would trample through the snow-covered woods and cut down the most enormous evergreen tree he could find for his sister and mother. And every year he removed his living room's picture window to accommodate that tree. Stan went to such extremes because they literally had hundreds of ornaments, each one more special than the next. It took them weeks just to decorate.

Therefore, I shouldn't complain when the repercussions of down-sizing invaded our holiday season again this year. When I pulled our old artificial Christmas tree out of storage, it looked way too big width-and length-wise for the family room. Therefore, I decided to put the tree up in the finished part of the basement where there was extra space. Not so good.

I started to assemble the three parts. I put the bottom section of the tree into the stand, then the middle piece. Lo and behold, I "hit the ceiling" when the third and final piece of the tree also hit the ceiling. It was a disaster in the making. Attaching the top of the tree, the most important part, into the midsection wasn't going to happen. It was squish-ville.

Also, how could our family be deprived of the yearly placement of the angel, which was positioned at the very top of the tree? To make matters worse, the angel was a gift, hand-stitched by my now deceased Aunt Dee.

I must admit, one holiday season I was naughty and substituted that angel with a picture of me instead.

Then there was the dilemma about the nativity scene. If there was no tree, where would the nativity scene be placed? This meant no room at Old Orchard Lane for Mary, Joseph and infant Jesus. What would Stan do?

In hindsight, when I went house hunting, maybe I should have bought a house to fit a tree. Or should I have bought a tree to fit the house? Frantic for solutions, my options were: making a special stand so the tree would sit horizontally instead of vertically, removing a basement ceiling tile allowing the whole tree to stand erect, or spending some bucks.

I've come to the realization that a smaller house means a smaller tree. The answer was buying a shorter, leaner, prelit tree. Sorry, Stan, I'm more the Charlie Brown type.

It's never easy for moms to let go

I have lived my entire life under the stigma of "be careful". Growing up, my mom kept a close eye on her children. Whenever I left her side and ventured off into the world, my mother would utter: "Karen be careful—watch both ways before you cross the street. Karen be careful—walk don't run. Karen be careful—it's getting dark." It wasn't until the first grade that I realized "Karen be careful" wasn't my real name.

Did "be careful" serve as an invisible safety net surrounding me whenever I wasn't within my mom's physical or emotional reach? My mother, Mary must have thought that "be careful" possessed some kind of medicinal powers, perhaps a notch below a "God bless you." Were those two little words as potent as holy water and capable of warding off evil spirits? Maybe my mom felt it counteracted her worried frame of mind and released her from the burden of responsibility if harm should come my way.

It started to get a little ridiculous when, as a teenager, my mother said, "Karen be careful" as I left the front stoop to retrieve the mail at the end of the driveway. But how could I complain when I returned seconds later without a scratch?

My mother needed to say those words because I was, in her own nice words, "quite active." For example, a nosy neighbor would call and inform my mom that she saw me throwing snowballs at passing cars, or riding my bicycle in traffic without any hands.

To this day, my mother won't reveal that neighbor's identity. But I have a hunch who tattletaled because that person's call backfired one evening: "Mary, I found your dog, filthy—covered in mud—I had to give him two baths."

"That's funny," my mom said, "because my dog is right here in the kitchen with me."

On my mom's 85th birthday, she revealed a secret about my first job. Some 30-plus years ago, I was a nurse in training and hired to work at a hospital during the summer in Cleveland, which was a three-hour trip. It might as well have been the end of the world, for my mother uttered "be careful" at least 20 times before she and my dad said their goodbyes.

My mom recently confessed that after they drove away, she had pleaded with my dad to turn around and take me back home.

"She'll be alright. Just leave her alone," were my father's words. Thinking back, I'm glad my father had so much confidence in me, or was it the gas mileage he was most concerned about?

Anyway, I survived and came back with new knowledge and a heightened dose of self-confidence. As a triage nurse in the emergency room, I had witnessed a patient suffer a heart attack before my very eyes and was able to institute the first steps of CPR by screaming, "Doctor—help!" I even diagnosed a patient's rising and falling abdomen as a possible aneurysm about to rupture.

Little did I realize, until her birthday confession, that my mom was so distraught upon leaving me in a bad section of town that she had actually consulted her family physician.

In retrospect, I feel extremely guilty about sending a concocted letter accusing her of desertion, and blaming her for all unbearable living and working conditions that I had endured while away, especially since it was written on the hospital's child-abuse form. She kept the letter.

Sorry, mom, I'll be more careful in the near future.

Unconditional love is a wonderful thing

Why do I love my dog more than family members? The reasoning is simple. I never get any complaints from Tanner. I have been feeding him the same dry dog food for breakfast and dinner for the past three years. And he still appreciates it, as if I made it special just for him. Add a little water to it and he's in doggone heaven.

This is in direct contrast to when I prepare people food. I often hear, "Not this again." Even when I try a new recipe it's, "This chicken tastes different. I don't like it. Can we order out?"

Another explanation is that Tanner doesn't talk back. Ask a teenager to do something and It's excuse-ville. Ask my dog to do something and he might not get it right, but he at least he tries. Tell him to sit, he lies down. Tell him to lie down, he sits.

It's a good thing dogs don't talk because he would probably hound me a thousand times a day - "take me for a walk" or "throw the ball, throw the ball, throw the ball." And how could I refuse someone who thinks I'm the greatest master in the whole wide world?

It appears that my dog's main goal in life is to please me, his caregiver. When I first got married, I thought that was the role of my husband. But after six months, the honeymoon was over. Does my husband of 20 years drool with anticipation when I enter our home? I don't think so. It's, "Hi Hon, what's for dinner?"

Tanner, on the other hand, sits like a sentinel at the front window happily awaiting my return home from work. As my car pulls into the driveway, Tanner can hardly contain himself. His body is in "per-pet-ual" motion, swaying from head to tail in joyful bliss. He brushes his body up against mine and bestows copious amounts of affection. It doesn't matter if I've been gone five minutes or five hours. It's the same welcome.

My dog has taught me a most important life lesson. When I gaze into his eyes, I see what my soul should be - unconditional love. Tanner judges me not, and loves me whether I'm happy, angry, sad, or mean.

History suggests that dogs were one of the earliest domesticated animals. I think they've got it reversed. It is my belief that dogs first domesticated humans a mere 55 million years ago, for I'd do anything for my dog and probably have.

It's too bad that I only have the remnants of a tailbone, which evolution decided to phase out. The human race would have been better off if we had kept our tails and the "spirit of wagging" alive.

If Tanner could speak, he'd admit that a person's character is determined not by appearance, words or monetary success, but on how well he treats his pets.

It's true I've given my dog lots of attention, taking him for romps in the woods and talking affectingly to him, which has invoked a response from my daughter. "Who do you love more, Tanner or me?"

"Why you, of course," was my reply. "Did you know that God spelled backward is dog. But don't worry; God corrected that slip-up at creation."

I further explained that when God created Adam and Eve, He chased them out of the Garden of Eden because they ate of the forbidden fruit, an apple. While running away, Adam tossed the apple aside. Unfortunately, Eve's pet dog thought that the apple was a red ball and also bit into it. Zap! God created cats. But that's another tail.

A little laughter helps lighten the tension

I spent 40 years as an operating room nurse trying to suppress my funny side in the arena of a sterile environment. This is not healthy. I had to bite my tongue so many times that my swollen tongue didn't fit in my mouth anymore. Good thing I wore a mask. But sometimes, the urge proved to be too much.

It all started in the lab at nursing school when I named my hairless cadaver cat, "Fluffy." Sometimes I can take things back. But not my nursing bandage scissors, which got flushed down a hospital toilet. In retrospect, I probably didn't want them back anyway.

Being a rookie had its ups and downs. For example, being sent by a surgeon to fetch a non-existent instrument called an "Otis elevator."

Surgeons don't like new faces in their OR, so when I entered the operating room where urologic surgery was being performed, the surgeons glared at me as if to say: What are you doing here? I quickly exited, but not before saying, "I'm just a kidney stone passing through."

There is a fine line when jokes in an operating room may or may not be funny. I had to take into consideration the severity of the procedure the patient was about to endure and whether the patient had a sense of humor. If not, I had to wait until the patient's pre-op sedation had taken effect. Could I refrain from telling the patient he would end up being a "numb skull" after receiving multiple local injections on his scalp? Maybe.

The holding area in the operating room is where patients are subjected to a list of questions to connect the right patient with the correct procedure. This is not the time to be funny, or is it?

Sometimes it is not what you say but how you say it that can get tricky. After verifying a patient's name and birth date according to his name tag, don't ask, "We are operating on your left knee—right?" Correct me if I'm wrong.

"Oops" is a word that is frowned upon in the operating room. I remember the time I unintentionally finished an operation before it even got started. A surgeon gave me an order to prep a small lesion on a patient's finger before he did his own cleansing. "Oops!" As I was scrubbing the lesion, it literally fell off. Did I have the nerve to ask the surgeon if he would split the bill with me? Yes, but no.

There are also some nasty odors in the operating room. A perforated bowel or a gangrenous limb is high on the list. So when a horrendous smell filled the hallways for days, we thought it was a diseased body part that never made it to the specimen lab. Much to our relief, discovered at the bottom of a trash can was someone's discarded broccoli. I knew the perpetrator, so when I came upon a broccoli refrigerator magnet, it had her name written all over it.

In the operating room, a certain level of quiet is maintained. Then again, there was that time when a scrub tech pushing a table filled with trays of heavy, dirty instruments into the hall lost control. A loud crash was followed by dead silence. The next thing I knew, I had blurted into the intercom, "Pick up on aisle one."

I wasn't sure if it was the clanging of metal instruments hitting the floor or my timely outburst that made the nursing supervisor exit his office expeditiously. I have since retired.

• • •